ALL ABOUT THE
OLD ENGLISH SHEEPDOG

Also available in this series

ALL ABOUT THE BASSET HOUND

ALL ABOUT THE BEAGLE

ALL ABOUT THE BULL TERRIER

ALL ABOUT THE GERMAN SHEPHERD DOG (ALSATIAN)

ALL ABOUT OBEDIENCE TRAINING FOR DOGS

ALL ABOUT POODLES

ALL ABOUT THE BOXER

ALL ABOUT THE COCKER SPANIEL

ALL ABOUT THE COLLIE

ALL ABOUT CROSS-BREEDS AND MONGRELS

ALL ABOUT THE DACHSHUND

ALL ABOUT THE GOLDEN RETRIEVER

ALL ABOUT THE YORKSHIRE TERRIER

In preparation

ALL ABOUT THE SHETLAND SHEEPDOG

ALL ABOUT THE
OLD ENGLISH SHEEPDOG

Jean Gould

PELHAM BOOKS

First published in Great Britain by PELHAM BOOKS LTD
52 Bedford Square, London, W.C.1
AUGUST 1973
SECOND IMPRESSION NOVEMBER 1974
THIRD IMPRESSION FEBRUARY 1976

ISBN 0 7207 0619 X

Printed in Great Britain by
Hollen Street Press Ltd at Slough, Berkshire
and bound by James Burn at Esher, Surrey

*This book is dedicated to my family
who never cease to tease me
that they come a very good second to the dogs*

ACKNOWLEDGEMENTS

My most grateful thanks to my daughter Wendy Gould for supplying the drawings and to my good friend John Featherstone for his delightful cartoons. Also I wish to express my gratitude to Mr Michael Garnett for his help and to my friends who so kindly supplied photographs, including the old and treasured photographs lent by Miss Florence Tilley and Mrs Mabel Gibson. My thanks are also due to Professor Lawson, for the invaluable help he afforded me with regard to diagrams relating to Hip Dysplasia.

CONTENTS

ILLUSTRATIONS

ACKNOWLEDGEMENTS

The author's grateful thanks are due to the following whose photographs are reproduced in this book: *Diane Pearce:* 1, 12; *Sport & General:* 11; *Anne Cumbers:* 13; *William P. Gilbert:* 15; *Johnnie Mc-Millan:* 16; *David Grimwade:* 19; *Press Association:* 20; *Marc Henrie:* 21.

LINE DRAWINGS

I

THE BOBTAIL

For the majority of dog lovers there is one particular breed which appeals and would-be owners set out to find a puppy of their choice, but this is not how 'Lassie', my first Old English Sheepdog, came to me when I was a schoolgirl. Training as a farm worker, Lassie did well until at two years old she refused to bark when rounding up the sheep. The owners, who could not afford a dog that did not work properly, were going to shoot her but luckily I heard about this and was able to save her from an untimely end. It is true that initially there was rather a cool reception on the part of my family for this large, knotted, muddy animal, loping along at the end of a chain and looking rather like an ill-kempt bear, but once the worst knots were cut off and I had bathed, fed and generally cared for her, she transformed into the most adorable and obedient dog it was ever my pleasure to own. Lassie was devoted to me and my family and we all adored her. She taught us to appreciate the truly endearing qualities of the breed which include a high intelligence, willingness to please, keen sense of fun, gentleness and patience, combined with a strong sense of duty as a guard.

The origin of the Old English Sheepdog remains obscure in spite of various investigations into the matter over the years, though a similar type of dog appears in paintings of the fifteenth century by Dürer and Van Eyck and there is a Gainsborough painting dated 1771 of the Earl of Buccleuch with a dog of this early type. From photographs of dogs of years gone by it appears that they were generally less heavily coated than those of present day, with much less head coat and featherings on the legs. Most of them were probably a little smaller in size.

The Russian Owtchar has been suggested as an ancestor and is of similar type though very much larger, being up to 30 or 32 inches at the shoulder. Without any close trading ties between Russia and Britain, it is difficult to imagine how this could have happened. The characteristic rolling gait of the Old English Sheepdog and the fact that it is formed with the hindquarters higher than the shoulder gave rise to the theory that there is a similarity to a bear and that bears must have had an influence on the breed. I think this highly unlikely and one could go on theorising without avail. The fact that various countries have similar types of sheepdog, including the French Briard and the Italian Maremma as well as the Russian Owtchar, may be due to the choice being made in the various countries independently for a squarely built dog with a guarding instinct, large and powerful enough to keep wolves and other wild beasts at bay. In the absence of proof, we shall never know whether there is any common blood between the sheepdogs of these other countries and our own breed.

In the eighteenth century, working dogs had their tails docked right off, or bobbed, as a sign that they were working dogs and not eligible to tax, and no doubt this is the reason the Old English Sheepdog is often referred to as the Bobtail. On rare occasions a puppy of this breed is born without a tail but usually they have long tails at birth which have to be removed surgically when 3 or 4 days old. There are accounts of bobtails being used years ago by drovers taking cattle or sheep to Smithfield and for this they must have been very hardy to go for many miles keeping up a steady pace. Although there is no longer this kind of work there are bobtails to be found on farms throughout the country. They are easy to train and undertake a variety of duties as, for instance, one bitch belonging to a neighbour of mine worked among poultry at the farm and it was a joy to watch the quiet and efficient way she would go to work putting the turkeys in their houses. She reached up to get those roosting in the trees and would make sure every single one was safely housed before trotting off to her next chore. She never nipped a bird and she worked silently so that the birds obeyed without being frightened.

The will to work is present in practically all bobtails. I am not the only breeder to have disproved the thought that show specimens are bred so highly for showing they forget the work they were intended to do. By taking various of my show dogs out to see what kind of a job they would make of fetching in our modest bunch of a dozen or so store cattle, I have found that without exception they have a very good sense of what is required and are trained easily. Some are quicker to learn that they must herd all the cattle and not pick out one single one, but it is to be expected in any group that some will be quicker than others to do it correctly.

It is interesting to watch an Old English Sheepdog going for a walk with several members of a family, for if the dog is running free and some of the party are walking a distance ahead, the dog will run to and fro and often push into the humans as it would into sheep, in an attempt to herd its family together.

A working dog should have a strong protective instinct, looking after sheep and lambs and keeping off marauders, and this would account for the bobtail's excellent qualities as a guard. I have known a number of them allow a trespasser in, only to corner them and refuse to let them out. This is very much more disconcerting to the intruder than a flat refusal of entry! This does not mean that they are fierce unless the need arises and most of them will guard a young child with a gentleness that has to be seen to be believed.

There are dogs of some breeds with high intelligence which they use mainly to gain their own ends, but sheepdogs in general and certainly the bobtail more often have a strong wish to please their master and devote their life to looking after him. In this connection an interesting case was reported in the national press a few years ago describing how the owner of an Old English Sheepdog was using petrol and he spilled this on his clothing, which caught fire and enveloped him in flames. Instantly his dog jumped at him, knocking him to the ground, then, whilst he was lying there, the dog proceeded to roll on the flames, putting out the fire. It was a very brave and intelligent action, presumably instinctive, and certainly saved the man's life.

Another instance of unselfish help concerns our family and bobtail taking a picnic in some woods about 25 miles from home on a sunny spring day when there was a bitterly cold wind. The children were playing some game during which one of them climbed along the branch of a tree overhanging a pool. The branch broke and we found ourselves with a soaking wet, shivering child, with all clothes not only saturated but covered in an evil smelling slime and the only course was to strip them off. As soon as that child climbed into the car covered only by a spare mackintosh, our bobtail jumped up and spread herself over the child as if warming an orphan lamb. Naturally we drove straight home and so successfully did the dog warm the child, that no harm came of the adventure, not even a sniffley head cold.

Some time ago I talked to a trainer from the Guide Dogs for the Blind Association at Exwick, for I knew the litter sister to the dog in the above story trained at Exwick. Owing to the grooming required for the heavy coat of a bobtail, the breed is not normally used for guide dogs, but at Exwick they have trained at least one dog and one bitch. The trainer said they were very quick to learn and made reliable guides. It is interesting to note that one dog trained as it is usual to use only bitches.

None of the dogs of my breeding have gone to train as guide dogs, but being interested in the cause, I used to collect money or sell raffle tickets for the Guide Dogs for the Blind Association, taking my dogs with me to attract attention to the good cause. It is surprising how much more response one gets when the dog is there to help on collecting days for they have only to sit and look friendly and beautiful and along come the people; so many people cannot resist talking to the dog and then they can scarcely refuse to support the cause.

The Old English Sheepdog is listed at the Kennel Club among Britain's Big Breeds and, properly groomed, must surely be among the most beautiful. It was one of the earlier breeds to appear at dog shows and in 1873 there was a class for the breed at Birmingham Show. Registrations at the Kennel Club have varied over the years; during the war years it was only a few of the dedicated breeders who managed to keep any stock at all and after the war the numbers picked up for a time but only 94 were registered in 1957. Then gradually there was an increase and in 1963 the number was 274. Between 1963 and 1970 the breed became more popular and numbers increased rapidly with 1970 seeing 2,343 dogs registered at the Kennel Club. In 1971 there was a further increase with 2,896 dogs registered and for the first time the Old English Sheepdog figured in the top twenty breeds registered at the Kennel Club; in the list giving the order they were 19th.

The Old English Sheepdog Club was founded in 1888 and some years after that the Committee of this Club compiled a Breed Standard which has remained unchanged ever since, and reads as follows:

SKULL. Capacious and rather squarely formed, giving plenty of room for brain power. The parts over the eyes should be well arched and the whole well covered with hair.

JAW. Fairly long, strong, square and truncated. The stop should be well defined to avoid a deerhound face. The attention of judges is particularly called to the above properties, as a long, narrow head is a deformity.

EYES. Dark or wall eyes are to be preferred.

NOSE. Always black, large and capacious.

TEETH. Strong and large, evenly placed and level in position.

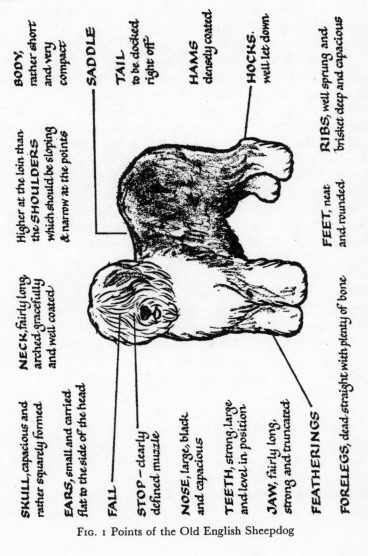

BODY, rather short and very compact

SADDLE

TAIL to be docked right off

HAMS densely coated

HOCKS well let down

RIBS, well sprung and brisket deep and capacious

Higher at the loin than the SHOULDERS which should be sloping & narrow at the points

FEET, neat and rounded

NECK, fairly long, arched gracefully and well coated

SKULL, capacious and rather squarely formed

EARS, small and carried flat to the side of the head

FALL

STOP—clearly defined muzzle

NOSE, large, black and capacious

TEETH, strong, large and level in position

JAW, fairly long, strong and truncated

FEATHERINGS

FORELEGS, dead straight with plenty of bone

FIG. 1 Points of the Old English Sheepdog

EARS. Small and carried flat to the side of the head, coated moderately with hair.

LEGS. The forelegs should be dead straight, with plenty of bone, removing the body a medium height from the ground without approaching legginess, well coated all round.

FEET. Small round, toes well arched and pads thick and round.

TAIL. Puppies requiring docking should have the operation performed within a week of birth, preferably within four days.

NECK AND SHOULDERS. The neck should be fairly long, arched gracefully and well coated with hair, the shoulders sloping and narrow at the points, the dog standing lower at the shoulders than at the loin.

BODY. Rather short and very compact, ribs well sprung and brisket deep and capacious. The loin should be very stout and gently arched whilst the hindquarters should be round and muscular, and with well let down hocks, and the hams densely coated with a thick long jacket, in excess of any other part.

COAT. Profuse and of good hard texture, not straight, but shaggy and free from curl. The undercoat should be a waterproof pile when not removed by grooming or season.

COLOUR. Any shade of grey, grizzle, blue or blue-merle, with or without white markings, or in reverse, any shade of brown or sable to be considered distinctly objectionable and not to be encouraged.

HEIGHT. Twenty-two inches and upwards for dogs, slightly less for bitches. Type, symmetry and character of the greatest importance, and on no account to be sacrificed to size alone.

GENERAL APPEARANCE. A strong, compact looking dog of great symmetry, absolutely free of legginess or weaselness, profusely coated all over, very elastic in its gallop, but in walking or trotting he has a characteristic ambling or pacing movement. His bark should be loud with a peculiar 'pot-casse' ring in it. Taking him all round he is a thick set, muscular, able-bodied dog with a most intelligent expression, free of all poodle or deerhound character.

SCALE OF POINTS
Total : 100

Head	5	Nose	5
Eyes	5	Teeth	5
Colour	10	Legs	10
Ears	5	Neck & shoulders	10
Body, loin & hind-		Coat	15
quarters	20	Jaw	10

About the time that the Old English Sheepdog Club was formed in England, we are told that the first specimens of the breed were imported into America. One of the founder members of our Club and great pioneer of the breed both here and in America was the late Mr H. A. Tilley, who was in partnership with his brother at Shepton Mallet in Somerset. In 1903 the Tilley Brothers took a team of bobtails to America and showed them at the Westminster Show. Mr Tilley's enthusiasm did much to fan the flame of interest in the breed in America and in 1905 the Old English Sheepdog Club of America came into being. It is interesting to note that Mr Tilley was a founder member of this Club in America as well as being a founder member of the Club in England.

The Breed Standard as laid down by the Old English Sheepdog Club of America is worded identically to that in this country, with the following exceptions :

EYES. Vary according to the colour of the dog. Very dark preferred, but in the glaucous or blue dogs a pearl, wall or china eye is considered typical. (A light eye is most objectionable.)

EARS. Medium sized and carried flat to side of head, coated moderately.

TAIL. It is preferable that there should be none. Should, however, never exceed one and a half or two inches in grown dogs. When not natural-born bobtails, however, puppies should be docked at the first joint from the body and the operation performed when they are from three to four days old.

BODY. Rather short and very compact, ribs well sprung and brisket deep and capacious. Slab-sidedness highly undesirable. The loin should be very stout and gently arched, while the hindquarters should be round and muscular and with well let down hocks, and the hams densely coated with a thick long jacket in excess of any other part.

COAT. Profuse, but not so excessive as to give the impression of the dog being over-fat, and of a good hard texture; not straight, but shaggy and free from curl. Quality and texture of coat to be considered above mere profuseness. Softness or flatness of coat to be considered a fault. The undercoat should be a waterproof pile, when not removed by grooming or season.

COLOUR. Any shade of grey, grizzle, blue or blue-merle, with or without white markings or in reverse. Any shade of brown or fawn to be considered distinctly objectionable and not to be encouraged.

GENERAL APPEARANCE AND CHARACTERISTICS. A strong, compact-looking dog of great symmetry, practically the same in measurement from shoulder to stern as in height, absolutely free from legginess or weaselness, very elastic in his gallop, but in walking or trotting he has a characteristic ambling or pacing movement, and his bark should be loud, with a peculiar 'pot-casse' ring in it. Taking him all round, he is profusely, but not excessively coated, thick-set, muscular, able-bodied dog with a most intelligent expression, free from all poodle or deerhound character. Soundness should be considered of greatest importance.

SCALE OF POINTS
Total : 100

Skull	5	Body & loins	10
Eyes	5	Hindquarters	10
Ears	5	Legs	10
Teeth	5	Coat (texture, quality	
Nose	5	& condition)	15
Jaw	5	General appearance &	
Foreface	5	movement	15
Neck & shoulders	5		

Although the American total of 100 points is allocated differently from the total of 100 points over here, the headings of the standard are identical. It is only to show the slight difference in the wording describing the breed requirements that the foregoing paragraphs have been quoted. The ultimate dog fitting the Breed Standard, whether English or American, would be much the same.

In America, as in England, there has been a very rapid increase in the breed since about 1960 and whilst this popularity is good in some ways, it can only be a benefit to the breed if breeders keep in mind that they must ever be striving to improve the breed and to give due consideration to what is required to keep a high standard. If indiscriminate breeding occurs and quantity rather than quality is turned out then the present popularity could be the downfall of this lovely breed. Good breeding passes on to the progeny and poor breeding also passes down for generations, with any faults arising from it taking years to eradicate by selective breeding.

It has been stated that soon after the Old English Sheepdog Club was founded in England in 1888 the Breed Standard was compiled and has remained unchanged, but for many years the wording regarding colour has been considered ambiguous, '. . . with white markings or in reverse' presumably could mean a dog with blue head and white body though this peculiarity is unlikely to occur. The Committee of the Club has therefore reviewed the description of colour and at the Annual General Meeting of the Club in March 1972 it was agreed to submit the following wording to the Kennel Club for approval: 'Any shade of grey, grizzle or blue-merle with white head, forequarters and hocks, with or without blue markings on the white parts. Any shade of brown or sable to be considered objectionable and any flashes in the blue body colour to be discouraged.'

2

CHOOSING A PUPPY

The important task of choosing a puppy is not an easy one particularly for the newcomer to the breed. Ideally it requires experience of handling young puppies and good adults, coupled with an 'eye' for recognising something good which shows promise for the future. For someone with no experience, buying a puppy for the first time, I advise them to begin by studying the Breed Standard set out in the previous chapter and to go to some of the shows; Championship shows if possible because at Championship shows there will be classes for the breed as a rule and a number of Old English Sheepdogs to be seen and compared. At Open shows there are sometimes a few classes for the breed but the entry would not be anything like the Championship entry, whilst at Limited shows it is doubtful if there would be any bobtails present. One really wants the opportunity of seeing a good entry of dogs in order to see what the winning dogs look like, in order to get a picture in mind of a good bobtail.

The next thing to do is to go to a reputable breeder who knows how to make a careful choice of stud for the bitch and who will follow that by good feeding and care of the inwhelp bitch and later of the puppies. There are numerous breeders who have the good of their breed at heart and who produce good healthy stock, but it is also possible to be 'sold a pup' in any breed as there are unfortunately some people who are stupid and unkind enough to turn out many litters of puppies from a bitch, without letting her recover her resources between litters and mostly they economise in feeding, just wanting a quick profit. I have seen a number of these undernourished puppies often with kind owners, who deserve something better, for once a puppy has had a bad start in life, the owners can only improve its condition. It is never possible to make up for that early lack of goodness and care. Often these puppies who get such a poor beginning in life are sold through commercially-minded dealers who trade in all popular breeds and there is no doubt the rapid increase in dog breeding in the past decade is responsible for the existence of these dog factories. Remembering that puppies are living creatures and have feelings and an intelligent mind, it is a terrible abuse to handle them so commercially. If the increase of dog breeding has caused a boom in dog products such as food, nylon bones and play things or equipment, that is fine, but a puppy needs love and individual attention. A reputable breeder takes pride in breeding something good and will lavish great care and attention on any stock they look after and certainly would be unwilling to sell to those dealers who sell indiscriminately. For this reason dealers of this kind tend to get poorly-reared puppies from equally commercially-minded breeders.

Whether the puppy is required for showing and breeding or just for a pet, it is therefore sensible to go to a reputable breeder who can offer a well reared puppy from good healthy stock. If you do this, it is unlikely that you will find a puppy with running eyes, or pot-bellied from incorrect feeding or worms, or one suffering from rickets, as you want to avoid these things at all costs; also, you should not find a puppy with fleas or other parasites from a good clean kennel. We will assume you are choosing from a healthy, bright eyed litter, firmly formed and with good, strong bone structure.

It may not occur to you to look for an umbilical hernia, but there may be one even in the best of litters. This appears like a little bubble in the middle of the abdomen and if the puppy lies on its back the bubble will go down. Usually as the puppy grows, the hernia reduces and never gives any trouble, but should you choose a puppy with a little hernia and you are at all worried about it, consult your Veterinary Surgeon. It is a very simple matter to have it stitched neatly across, if he considers it necessary.

It is a good idea to see the parents of the puppy if this is possible, in order to find out their temperament as well as their looks. One point to mention here is that the puppies in the nest will not resemble their parents in colour as they are blue/black – known as blue – and white when born. The white parts will remain white, but the blue will begin to change to a pale blue/grey at about three or four months, and between three months and about eighteen months the coat will have changed to a very pale colour all over, except for the white markings. Gradually the very pale coat will tend to darken until the adult bobtail will end up some shade of blue, grey or merle which is very much darker than the second coat. This applies to the average bobtail but there are exceptions such as the dog that casts its puppy coat only to grow an adult coat that is more or less as dark, the final colour being a clergyman grey. Other coats stay very pale and look a kind of washed out colour, but the majority of coats follow the normal pattern whether they are quick to change or very slow to change.

There is a condition known as hip dysplasia which occurs in some Old English Sheepdogs as in other large breeds, but except in very extreme cases, it is not possible to diagnose in very young puppies by watching them move about. More explanation will be given of this condition in a later chapter, but when buying a puppy, it is an advantage if the breeder is in the habit of having stock X-rayed before it is bred from, to find out whether the hip joints are sound. As hip dysplasia is considered to be a hereditary defect, there should be less risk of having this trouble in the puppy if the parents are X-rayed and found to be clear.

On no account choose a frightened little thing that backs away; the ones that come forward full of curiosity and friend-

liness, with a bold outlook on life will be much easier to
handle later on. For a family pet simply choose the puppy
that is bold and that appeals to you; or, it may well be that
as the puppies play about, you will find one following closely
and making it clear it is choosing you!

Much more thought must be given when choosing a puppy
destined for the show ring as there are so many points to
consider. If you want a dog then shut away the bitches, or
shut away the dogs if you want a bitch, as it gets confusing
with eight or nine running around, but if you are undecided
whether to have a dog or a bitch then you will have to start
with the whole litter. In any case it is easiest to sort them by
elimination though for the first five minutes they will probably all look alike and equally adorable. Whilst they play
about, you should note the bigger heads and square bodies.
Eliminate any narrow heads or long-bodied puppies. Some
markings are more attractive than others but the main object
is to have a well made, sound puppy, well off for bone and
moving truly; one with straight forelegs and with hindlegs
showing no sign of 'cow hocks' (when they are too close at
the hocks). For correct hocks, which should turn neither in
or out, see Fig. 2.

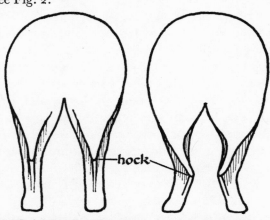

STRAIGHT HOCKS   COW HOCKS
Fig. 2 Hocks

Look for a good reach of neck and this can be measured by closing your fist gently around the neck. When I measure with my fist, I find a very good neck on an eight week puppy is when there is just room for the width of my hand when it closes around the neck, but on an average length neck there is not quite room to accommodate my hand. According to the width of your hand you will learn to feel when it is a good neck.

Another important point to watch for is the mouth which on examination should have the jaws and teeth with correct bite; that is, with the front top teeth fitting snugly just over the top of the teeth of the bottom jaw. The illustrations in Fig. 3 show a correct bite and various incorrect bites.

Eyes should be dark brown or 'wall', the latter is a term describing a blue eye and can be referred to as glaucose, pearly grey or a 'china eye'. A wall eye in a young puppy is usually bright blue but later it pales to a light blue/grey and the outside rim of the colour is even paler, almost white in some cases. The dog can have one dark eye and one wall, or both eyes the same colour, but whatever you do be sure to avoid light brown eyes. There is a school of thought that there must not be two wall eyes but if this is so all I can say is that I well remember Mrs M. N. Gibson's Ch. Beckington Tom Tod, who had two of the best wall eyes I have ever seen, getting his 18th Challenge Certificate. If there is a little pigmentation surrounding the eyes, it is a good point as, providing it has some black dots of pigmentation, these will increase and if you are lucky there will be a dark circle right around the eye. The circle of pigmentation gives a good setting to the eye but if a good dog has lovely dark eyes with little or no pigmentation it will not be 'thrown out with the rubbish'. Good pigmentation generally is desirable and many puppies have their noses completely black when they are eight weeks old, but others may take a little longer to fill in and may still have pink speckles at that age which must turn black. I remember one sweet little bitch whose mistress

CORRECT BITE

SCISSOR

INCORRECT BITES

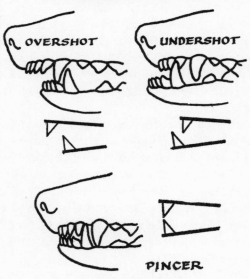

OVERSHOT UNDERSHOT

PINCER

Fig. 3 The bite

was afraid her nose would never be completely black as it had some pink speckles when I saw her at eighteen months, but in time it did turn completely black and I have never known a nose that did not eventually fill in. For breeding purposes it is not wise to choose a puppy that has unusually slow pigmentation on the nose. Many dogs have a pink rim to the eye all their life and they will not be penalised for this providing it is a good dark eye, but the setting and expression of the eye is much improved with a dark rim and a wall eye looks very lacking if there is no pigmentation.

Some people in our neighbourhood bought a bobtail puppy and when I saw it at ten weeks there was no pigmentation around either of the eyes. A few months later they asked me to come and see the puppy and they were on the point of going to the Veterinary Surgeon for advice as a black mark had appeared on the eye lid and they thought it some kind of blemish. I assured them this was a mark of beauty and I hoped there would be more black around the eyes in future!

Remember the muzzle should not be long or pointed; it should be square looking. Ears should be neatly at the side of the head and not set too high up on top of the head. Another point is the shape of the body which, when you look down on it, should be pear shaped, being wider and higher at the rear than at the shoulder.

After considering the foregoing points, you will have eliminated a number of puppies and there may remain two or three which are good enough for your choice; the thing to decide is which puppy has most virtues and no faults. Comparing the final two or three, look at the hindlegs and see if the point of hock is high up or low down on the leg. If it is high, the lower joint will be rather straight like a Chow and this is not what is required, choose one well let down at the hock as shown in Fig. 4.

If the decision is difficult because one is better this way and another that, then markings may help with the final choice. It has been fashionable in recent years to show dogs with an all white head and front, whereas years ago the old type of bobtail was heavily marked more often than not, having blue ears and masks around the eye and bands of blue around the top of the forelegs to mention just a few of the darker markings. It is preferable to have a white collar which is continuous all around the neck because when the dog is looked at on a side where the blue of the body continues

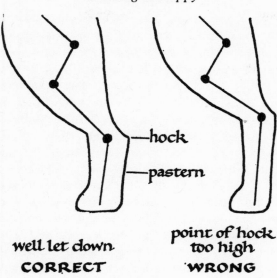

well let down
CORRECT

point of hock
too high
WRONG

FIG. 4 Hind leg

right up to the ear or face, with no white to break it up, one gets the impression of a long dog, therefore it is better to avoid this if possible. White forelegs with or without a band of blue and a white head with or without patches of blue, such as one mask or two masks, or blue ears or one blue ear, or a dot on the top of the head, all are perfectly acceptable and many of these blue markings are exceptionally attractive. It is amusing that, since there are so many white heads in the show ring today, I have been asked for a puppy suitable for showing and, if the one I am offering has a blue ear or mask, once or twice the purchaser has intimated that it was a pity the puppy had these marks as it would be no use in the show ring! This is quite wrong of course, and although I have shown a number of all-white headed dogs, I consider masks around the eyes most attractive and there are many other blue markings which help to give character to the dog.

There is a certain amount of controversy about mismarkings, but large white flashes in the blue coat on the back of the dog are not encouraged. Years ago, breeders put to sleep any puppies with a white flash on the back as it was considered to be a fault, but this is not often done nowadays if it is done at all as the demand for puppies has greatly increased and people are glad to have these puppies as pets. The only point is that, having bought the puppy as a pet, they may at a later stage decide to breed a litter and if the flashing is dominant, this is a pity as it will pass on to a percentage of the progeny for some generations. Providing the Kennel Club approve the new wording relating to colour in the Breed Standard, it will be apparent that white flashes in the blue body coat are to be discouraged and it is a good thing to clarify this point as the present wording is very ambiguous. A line of white hairs or a small mark in a young puppy's coat will show up as the blue is so dark and the white contrasts against it. However, usually this will grow out when the second coat comes through and it would be wrong to condemn a good puppy with a very small flash or little line of hairs. Since the breed began, the back of the Old English Sheepdog has been blue, grey or merle with adult coat and, if big patches of white on the back are accepted, in time the markings may become piebald. It is among the points to watch when breeding.

When you have eventually made the comparisons and chosen the puppy which pleases you, confirm from the breeder that it has been effectively wormed. After that, waste no time in consulting your Veterinary Surgeon regarding vaccination against the serious diseases of distemper, hard pad, hepatitis and leptospirosis, as the puppy should not mix with the outside world without this protection. Some Vets vaccinate at eight weeks of age and others at about twelve weeks according to which type of vaccine they use.

The breeder will provide you with a pedigree and, if the puppy has already been registered at the Kennel Club, you will get a registration certificate and form of transfer to complete and send to The Kennel Club, 1, Clarges Street, Piccadilly, London, W1Y 8AB, in order to have the puppy transferred to your name.

For those who have not handled a very young puppy before, I give a word about how to pick it up and carry it. Putting your hands either side of the puppy over the shoulders, slide one hand down behind the forelegs and bring it up to rest between the forelegs, whilst the other hand goes back to support the hindquarters. Once picked up a small puppy can be transferred to one arm, by resting its body on your arm with your hand supporting under the forelegs and your elbow supporting its hindquarters. Be sure to keep the puppy's elbows tucked in neatly. With a larger and heavier puppy, it will take two hands to hold it in more or less the position used to pick it up.

Public Transport presents a problem to Bobtailers...

Whilst you are flushed with excitement at acquiring such a beautiful specimen of the breed, do not be too discouraged if comparatively few people know what breed it is. When I acquired a beautiful bitch which was to be my first show dog, I was leading her out on one of her first walks when a man stopped to admire her. Standing back to get a good look at her, he paused for thought as he studied her and then said 'That's a nice puppy and I reckon there is a little bit of sheepdog in it somewhere.' Luckily I was too astonished at his ignorance to reply, as I might have been rather rude to him, but I must add that this puppy 'with a little bit of sheepdog in her somewhere' became my first Champion!

3

HOUSING

There is no problem for the owner of one dog in keeping it in the house, but being large and woolly, it is wise to have some place where the dog can go after a walk, especially if the weather is wet. In an old house there will probably be a back kitchen or outhouse but in a modern dwelling it is not so easy and use will have to be made of a porch or corner of a garage, unless there is a good shed.

After a walk on a wet day, I have found the quickest way to dry a bobtail is to get a bucket of warm water and a chamois leather, then spread out a newspaper on the floor and make the dog sit on it. Squeeze out the chamois and then rub the coat, particularly the tummy, legs and feet, and each time the chamois gets wet swill it in the water and squeeze it out again. This not only dries the dog but cleans it at the same time and very soon after this kind of drying the dog is clean and fit to come into the house. It is remarkable how quickly a dog, who is used to having its feet dried, will sit patiently and lift first one front paw and then the other for drying before standing so that the hindlegs can be done. Like most things in their doggy life, it is a matter of repetition which fixes the routine in their mind and trains them to be so bidable and helpful.

I have known several new owners make the mistake of letting a new puppy live in the house for the first three or four months, with the intention of putting it out in a shed when it is old enough, but this is bad policy because no dog will take kindly to the arrangement. It will have enjoyed having company and being with the family and will create no end of fuss. If the dog is ultimately to be housed in a shed, you should start as you mean to go on and let it learn to live in the shed right away and being young it should soon settle and accept this as its home. Only bring a puppy into the house to live if you intend to keep it there.

For the dog that is to live in the house as a family dog, there must be some place where it can sleep at night and rest peacefully when it wishes during the daytime. A puppy should begin by being introduced to a bed of its own and, being a large breed, if a large bed is available, it is a good plan to place a smaller temporary box inside the large bed for use until the puppy has grown. The bed should be raised a few inches from the ground to avoid draughts and is best sited in a quiet corner where the puppy will be disturbed as little as possible when resting. As the new puppy will miss his brothers and sisters, it gives comfort during the first few nights if a stone hot water jar is wrapped in a piece of blanket and put in the bed to give warmth and company. I usually heat it for a night or two and then leave it unheated as a kind of companion. If, however, the weather is exceptionally cold, or the puppy rather small for its age, the jar can be heated until it seems the warmth is no longer necessary.

For those of us who have more than one dog, it is necessary to give careful thought to the planning of the housing. Dogs like company and a double kennel housing a pair is useful, but a bitch in season or a bitch with puppies needs a single kennel. This should be roomy so that the dog can have space to move about and small enough to be cosy and there should be a raised platform to form a bed. If one is lucky enough to have suitable outbuildings which can be adapted, this will save an expensive outlay on new kennels, but unless there is something of this kind to adapt, it will be necessary to build a new kennels and the most usual thing to do is to buy wooden sheds.

The siting of the kennels is of great importance. One should try to make use of any walls or hedges to give some shelter and site the kennels facing away from the east wind; bearing in mind that in a very sheltered position a kennel facing due south will get very hot in summer sunshine and it would probably be better to have it facing west or north-west and arrange for some form of shade. On the other hand, in an exposed situation use must be made of all possible shelter and the kennel might be best facing south as it will need the warmth of the sun. One has to position the kennel so that the dog within does not suffer from extremes either of heat or cold; particularly a cold east wind. If it can be arranged that the site chosen is situated on well drained land, this will help to avoid wet and boggy runs and general dampness which would be bad for any dog and, whilst the shed or sheds are sited where the adults can be comfortably housed in all weathers, it must be kept in mind that any shed, intended for housing very young puppies to live in and to run about outside in their early days, will need warmth and sunshine.

Wooden sheds, which are soundly made and draught proof, make ideal kennels and if there is a lining of hard-board it will be easier to keep clean and provide a smooth surface which the dogs are unlikely to chew. It will also give good insulation. For a single kennel, a shed 9 ft. long and 5 ft. wide is suitable and it will need a wooden floor and a roof high enough for an average person to stand without getting a bump on the head. A wooden floor is as good as any type for cleanliness and is cosier than concrete, also when scrubbed it dries out fairly quickly. For a double kennel the length should be 10 ft. and the width about 6 ft. 6 in. In either of these sheds, apart from a wooden floor, there should be a platform raised about 4 in. from the floor which can fit across the back of the shed, running the full width of the shed and measuring 3 ft. in depth. Also a ledge about 4 in. high running across the front of the platform will help to keep the bedding in place. I say 'help' to keep it in place because one dog often decides to have a wild game in new bedding before lying down and settling in it, and when two dogs are kennelled together they are fairly sure to play about, especially if they are young. This is the joy of having company and being in the same kennel. It is certain that if wild games go on, not all the bedding will stay on the platform but usually there is enough left to make a comfortable bed.

Some kennels have the window and door on the same side of the building and in this case they are on one of the longer sides, but it is equally convenient to have the door on one of the shorter ends and the window on the longer side. Avoid placing a door at one end and window at the opposite end, because apart from being draughty, the dog usually likes to be able to retreat to the safety of the darker end of the shed to sleep, where there are solid walls and no disturbing influences. The window should be fairly large to give plenty of light and air and it is best sited quite low, say about 2 ft. 6 in. up from the floor for the bottom of the window, as a high window has the effect of making the dog jump up to look out. Too much jumping up and standing on the hindlegs is not considered good for the joints and in any case it is more pleasant for a dog to be able to take an interest in all that goes on, without having to peep from a high window. Unless the weather is bad and rain blowing in, there should always be an open window to let the dog have the benefit of fresh air and any sunshine. Windows opening outward and upward will give protection from rain and a section of chain link, as one uses for fences, should be fixed inside the window frame so that there is no way for the dog to escape or for another animal to jump in. It also gives protection to the window panes when the window is shut, or to any fixed panes. Some kennels have wooden shutters rather than glass window panes and metal bars across the frame; this is serviceable but the kennel is much darker when the shutters have to be across.

In some of our kennels instead of a hinged window there is a window space with the link fencing guard and on the outside of the shed are runners to accommodate glass shutters, which slide across when the weather is bad. This is a simple way of making ventilation and the glass shutters are so easy to adjust. The type of hinged window that opens upward certainly does help keep normal rain from entering the kennel, but living as we do near the coast, we are subjected to raging gales and wild conditions from time to time and a hinged window is in danger of being torn off altogether. For reasonably sheltered positions, the hinged window is probably the better type.

Inside the door of all our sheds, I have had a small door about 20 in. high fitted so that I can get in or out by stepping over, but puppies are kept safely inside and adult dogs are deterred from coming out, unless I open it for them to come out. Also it is useful to have a shelf which, among other things, will accommodate a tray of puppy feeds and thus save one the embarrassment of trying to balance the tray in one hand and put feed dishes down with the other. One needs a free hand to stop an eager puppy diving into the food.

In summer time there is no need for any bedding to give warmth as an Old English Sheepdog is more likely to be trying to keep cool in hot weather, but if the dog is left to lie down on a hard surface for any length of time, the elbows and hocks will suffer as the coat will be rubbed off with the weight of the dog lying down and with the impact as it comes down on a hard surface. This is less of a problem if there is a piece of carpeting on the platform to cushion the fall when the dog lies down. Very likely the dog will prefer to lie on the floor where it is cooler, but it is worth trying.

In winter time, when it is necessary to provide bedding, one of the best things to use is wheat straw; other types of straw can harbour parasites, but wheat straw is non-heating and usually very clean. Another good type of bedding is wood shavings.

It is a great advantage if it is possible to have an electric lead run across to the kennels both for lighting and for an infra red lamp for use when there are newly born puppies. The switch should be fixed high up and a little distance back from the door in order to be out of the way of dogs jumping up and turning on the light.

A strong utility bucket makes a useful container for drinking water in the kennel and if a board or bar is fitted across across one corner of the shed, the bucket can stand behind it and avoid being knocked over.

A shed of single size can be used for a bitch in whelp, but once the puppies are born, there is one more requirement to make the platform into a suitable box, and that is a board 5 ft. long and 18 in. high. Stand this board on the floor holding it tightly against the front of the platform and it can be bolted or screwed in three or four places to the 4 in. upright which keeps the bedding in place and is fixed on the front of the platform. As the platform is 4 in. off the ground and the front ledge is 4 in. high, the new board, being 18 in., will give an additional 10 in. of depth to the front of the bed and keep the whelps safely inside. The dam should find no difficulty in jumping in over that height.

When the puppies are old enough to want more room, they should be able to move freely about the shed and the board can be dismantled and put away until there is another new litter. At the same time it is wise to remove the complete platform from the shed and put deep bedding in its place. Even if the very young puppies could climb up on to the platform, the struggle would not be a good exercise for them as it would be harmful to their legs and shoulders. They require a very safe place on the level.

Having considered suitable kennelling, the next requirement is a good run adjoining the kennel. It is best that the dog can go from its kennel into the run and not have to be taken at set times to a run away from the kennel, even if it is only a short distance away. When a dog is left in its run, it will potter to and fro to the kennel, which is home to it, and if something frightens it the immediate reaction is to run home to safety. Also many dogs learn to go in the kennel in heavy rain or if it is too cold for lying about. I may add that there are almost as many dogs that will lie out in a down-pour of rain, surveying the scene as if it were a bright sum-mer day!

A dog that has had no knowledge of living anywhere but in a kennel will settle quite happily in a double kennel with a run, and with another dog as kennel mate. Some settle very well in a single kennel on their own though many find this lonely. Once they have settled and look on it as home, they can stay there permanently, but they miss human company and getting used to a variety of noises in the home and greeting friends who call at the door and generally having a wide education as to how to behave, quite apart from getting house trained. For this reason I settle young puppies out in a shed and then, when they are a little older and quite happy about the life, invite them indoors for a short while each day, during which time I see they get house trained. As they grow up they sometimes come in for more than one session a day, especially in winter time when they cannot spend as much time in their runs and it must be very boring being shut in a kennel for hours on end. If the dogs are not to be allowed in the house to relieve the monotony, they really need a covered run so that they will not have to be shut in except at night. This would make their life more interesting.

If a dog is to be allowed in the house with its family for the greater part of the day and is intended to use the kennel for night time and when the dog is drying after a wet outing, there is no need to make a run. However, for dogs which have to be kennelled permanently or for the majority of the time, the run must be as large and interesting as possible. Use can be made of any available walls or hedges, taking as much ground as can be spared and enclosing it with chain link fencing 6 ft. high. Upright posts set at intervals with the fencing attached and horizontals running across the top of the fencing to give strength, for the fencing will have to be strong to withstand the battering it will get from these large dogs who will be sure to jump up at times and throw their weight against it. I have experienced two bobtails who would not stay behind a 6 ft. fence; one never escaped whilst I was watching but as soon as my back was turned she was outside the run and following behind me and I suspect she scrambled up and over. The other more or less cleared it by jumping and scrambling over the top. However, normally a bobtail will stay behind a 5 ft. or 6 ft. fence.

There will have to be a gate and two strong posts will be necessary, one for hanging the gate and the other for it to fasten to. The gate fastening will have to be of a kind that the dogs cannot unfasten and I advise a bolt which can slide across and be made fast in position. I have known bobtails who are extraordinarily clever about opening fastenings, lifting hook fasteners, turning a large key, pressing a thumb latch or operating a lever-type door handle. The bolt is safest positioned outside the gate and if it is not possible to work the bolt from inside the gate, fix a small fastening inside as well so that the gate will be safely fastened behind anyone going into the run.

There are various opinions as to the ideal type of surface for a dog's run, some advocating earth with cinders to strengthen and give body to it, some advising concrete runs as being clean and they can be scrubbed down with disinfectant, others prefer grass. All concrete is not only uninteresting but it is hard for the pads of the feet and in time can cause sore pads, particularly in young puppies when the pads are more tender. All soft surface like grass is inclined to make the feet spread and the dog's nails grow too long. It is preferable to have a hard surface just outside the kennel, so that concrete forming a small yard which reaches to the gate will give enough hard surface and it is decidedly more pleasant when attending to the dogs as one does not get muddy feet when going to and fro. If the concrete has a slightly rough finish it will be good for feet and nails and will not be slippery as smooth concrete is. If the rest of the run is in grass it will not only look tidy but will be pleasant for the dogs to run about and find a certain amount of interest. Even if, with two dogs playing, the grass gets worn it never gets as muddy and dirty for them as plain soil or cinders.

If one is keeping a stud dog with several bitches, it is best to have him kennelled a distance away from them as it is better for his peace of mind when they come in season. If he is exercised in a direction away from the bitches at that time and kennelled away from the smell of them there is no need for him to be too worried and upset or to go off his food.

4

FEEDING

Having acquired a quality puppy, it is necessary to give the very best of food when rearing in order to make the bone and sturdy frame required and if it is to be a thoroughly healthy puppy, full of energy, with good teeth, a clear eye and healthy skin.

We know that originally in its wild state dog was a carnivore, that is, he was a flesh eating animal. He used to hunt his quarry to kill and eat it, therefore his chief natural food was raw flesh and no doubt he chewed many of the bones as well. Also, dog has always eaten a certain amount of vegetation and still today domesticated dog will take the opportunity to pick out and eat certain types of grasses when he gets the chance to find them in the fields and hedges.

After years of being domesticated, dog has learned to enjoy a varied diet and this should consist of protein and carbohydrates with vitamin and mineral supplements. Protein is found mainly in meat, eggs, fish and cheese, carbohydrates in biscuit meal and bread (given as brown bread baked or rusked), and vitamins will include Vitamins A, B, D and E, and there must be calcium and phosphorous.

A little fat should be included in the diet and this is assumed to be provided in the meat. If the dog has access to grass it will eat what it requires to get Vitamin C, as a blood purifier, otherwise green vegetables can be included in the diet.

Balancing the correct amount of vitamins and calcium and phosphorous is rather complicated and this is why it is much easier to use a comprehensive vitamin tablet which has been scientifically balanced and is ready to administer by giving according to the weight of the dog.

Much as been written about the intake of vitamin supplements of which Vitamins A, B, D and calcium and phosphorous are especially vital whilst the puppy is growing, for bitches in whelp and, to a lesser extent, for dogs in old age, but broadly speaking the main supplements are as follows :

Vitamins A and D are necessary for promoting growth, forming bone and preventing rickets, but it is important not to give more than the dose prescribed of Vitamin D.

Calcium and phosphorous are necessary, together in the correct ratio, to strengthen bone formation and these cannot be absorbed without the presence of Vitamin D.

Vitamin B is for strengthening of the nerves.

Vitamin E is for fertility.

The diet will have to be carefully planned and any idea that a dog should be allowed to eat until it has satisfied its hunger because Nature will see to it that the dog knows when to stop, is quite wrong. Regular well planned meals are essential to the dog's well being and one should bear in mind that over feeding is even more harmful than under feeding. A working dog will use up a great deal of energy and therefore require more food than a dog that is kept quietly doing little and using up very little energy.

For a puppy of 8 weeks, I recommend five feeds a day as follows :

7.30 a.m. ½ pint warm milk, 1 teaspoon glucose and cereal (Baby foods such as Farex, baby rice, Weetabix, porridge).

11.30 a.m. 6 oz. finely chopped meat and 2 heaped tablespoonfuls 'dry soaked' biscuit meal of puppy grade.

'Dry soaked' means with enough hot water

poured over the meal to soak in and not be sloppy. Puppy meal will have to soak for $\frac{1}{4}$ hour to penetrate thoroughly and larger grades of biscuit meal later on will have to soak for at least $\frac{1}{2}$ hour.

3.30 p.m. $\frac{1}{2}$ pint milk pudding (semolina, rice, etc., preferably made with the addition of an egg).

7.00 p.m. As at 11.30 a.m. with the addition of vitamins. Either give calcium in tablet or bone meal form, Cod Liver Oil and Vitamin B tablets, or give one of the comprehensive vitamin supplies which are manufactured in tablet form. The comprehensive tablets have calcium, phosphorous and minerals and vitamins all in the correct ratio, and the number of tablets given depends on the body weight of the puppy.

10.30 p.m. As at 7.30 a.m.

At 12 weeks increase the puppy biscuit meal quantities, also vitamins, but reduce to four meals instead of five.

At 18 weeks still gradually increasing the quantities at each meal, reduce to three meals per day.

At 24 weeks give two meals; the diet can now include suitable table scraps and the addition of a little vegetable oil is beneficial. Puppy grade biscuit can now be substituted by a larger grade and the total daily ration of meat should be at least $1\frac{1}{2}$ lb.

The amounts of food stated above are given as a guide for an average Old English Sheepdog, but some dogs will put on weight and thrive whereas others will eat well and yet stay too lean, particularly whilst growing. If this is the case, provided the dog has been successfully wormed and is not being over exercised, the meat can be increased gradually to 2 lb. per day after 24 weeks, plus as much biscuit meal as can be digested. Also give the food in three meals for a few more months by providing an extra meal at breakfast and then two meat and biscuit feeds later in the day. The breakfast can consist of boiled rice with an egg beaten in, fed when it has cooled; or it can be one of the foods advertised as a 'complete feed' which may need mixing with a little milk, or may be in the form of pellets, and should prove to be a help as a fattener when given in addition to the normal diet. It is bad to have a fat dog but when fast growing a large framed dog can be very thin and one has to work hard to rectify this.

A more difficult situation arises when a growing dog, or even an adult is thin because it will not eat heartily as most dogs do. A really faddy feeder is exasperating and there is no doubt that the more one panders to it the worse it becomes. I believe in trying a number of variations in the food in order to find out if there is anything at all that this dog will eat and appear to enjoy. One can try fish, eggs, cottage cheese, cooked meat, raw meat, minced meat and so on but having prepared a tempting meal, if the dog will not eat it, then pick it up and give nothing until the next meal. Sometimes the sense of competition with another dog, or even a cat, will make a dog eat even if not very keen on the food produced. Even if your dog is not a faddy feeder but a hearty eater, it will still appreciate variety in the diet, furthermore, no one feed contains absolutely all the essentials of a diet in sufficient quantities so that anything lacking slightly in one feed could very well be present in some item of another feed, therefore, a certain amount of variety in the diet is beneficial.

We have considered the thin dog and the faddy feeder but another exception is the dog that puts on weight too easily and this is very unusual when a young dog is fast growing; it is more common with adults. The meat ration can be reduced a little and 'dry soaked' biscuit meal replaced by a slice of baked brown bread, or liver rusks which are purported to be non-fattening and can be obtained at most pet shops. Also be sure the dog is getting sufficient exercise. However, having tried this, if the dog still puts on weight, it would be wise to consult your Veterinary Surgeon. It may be that there is nothing wrong with the dog and the fact that it puts on weight is due to it being a particularly 'good doer' – probably a dog with a very placid temperament – as this type will put on weight much faster than one which is nervous or highly strung, but I have known of cases of obesity in dogs which were traced to the dog having an underactive thyroid gland.

From six months to about two years, the dog needs to continue on the maximum amount of food, but once it has reached maturity the amount of food can be reduced a little. It is during the fast growing and developing stage that most intake of food is required. The average adult bitch being smaller than the dog, in most cases, will require between 1 lb. and $1\frac{1}{4}$ lb. meat per day and the average adult dog $1\frac{1}{4}$ lb. to $1\frac{1}{2}$ lb. meat per day. Old dogs will not require as much meat in their diet, the protein can be reduced and a diet arranged to include more eggs and fish instead of meat. Some old dogs put on weight and therefore want less meat and very little biscuit, but others lose weight in their later years and in this case one should include rice pudding, cereals, extra biscuit meal, etc., in the menu. An old dog also requires the addition of calcium either as bone meal or calcium tablets. It is amusing to notice how well an older dog will eat and even one, who in younger days was a faddy feeder, will perk up in old age and take great interest in food, waiting regularly at feed times, like some elderly pensioner at a boarding house, waiting for the dinner gong to sound!

Many adult dogs have only one meal a day, but I have found a few dogs who cannot digest sufficient food in one meal; it is less hard on the digestion to give a small midday meal and big main meal in the evening and I continue to give two meals in this fashion throughout the dog's life. The small midday meal helps to keep each dog at the correct weight as the thinner dogs get more and those inclined to over-weight get less, perhaps just a token such as a small crust of baked brown bread. Although dogs will wait around patiently, or in some cases impatiently for their feed and they come to no harm if it is served early or late, I feel it is fair to be reasonably punctual at each meal for the dog asks very little and feed time is one of the high spots of the day. Fix a feeding routine to suit yourself and your family and then try to keep to it.

There should always be a supply of clean drinking water available and for puppies it is best put in the same place always so that they know where to find it. As puppies are inclined to paddle in their drinking water and have a wet and messy game with it, be sure the water container is sited where it will not tip over. Any small drinking bowls provide a great game, as a puppy of six or seven weeks will pick a bowl up in its mouth with the water slopping in all directions and more often than not the bowl gets broken. For adults, as already mentioned, a strong utility bucket is ideal, but for puppies of six weeks and over a small bucket fixed firmly behind a board or bar in the corner of the kennel is safe from spilling and is low enough for them to reach for a drink.

As our dogs take turns in coming into the house with us and one very special character, Champion Rollingsea Snow Boots, lives in the house permanently, we have drinking water in the kitchen and dining-room and for this purpose a deep enamel pudding basin is clean and holds a reasonable amount of water. For the bowl in the dining-room I have bought a plant container in which to stand the enamel bowl and this is pleasant to look at and it saves any moisture from the bowl harming the carpet. As there are so many very attractive plant pot containers in the shops these days it is easy to choose one that looks decorative.

A dog should not be allowed to drink large draughts of water immediately after a meal or after violent exercise and it is advisable to remove the drinking water for a while at these times. If the dog is desperately thirsty give a very little drink and then pick up the water container until about an hour later.

Although the natural protein food for a dog is fresh meat, which is best given raw, it is not always easy to get a good supply of fresh meat and many owners give their dogs one of the 'complete feeds' on the market today and whether prepared as a coarse meal or in pellet form, they mostly claim to contain cereal flakes, meat or beef, fish, dried milk, vitamins and vegetable oil or linseed oil; though some manufacturers quote the calorie content. It is an alternative to buy cooked meat, or cooked meat and cereal deeply frozen or in tins. The inclusion of eggs, tripe or cottage cheese in the diet helps out with the meat ration and it should be noted that a 2 oz. egg has the same protein value as 4 ozs. of meat.

I have read articles in various dog books and periodicals regarding the effect on dogs of including raw eggs in the diet. In the white of an egg there is a substance called avidin which adversely affects the absorption of Biotin, a vitamin of the B complex, but once the egg is cooked the avidin is destroyed and the intake of Biotin is not affected. Some breeders therefore feel it necessary to cook eggs, by hard boiling or scrambling, when including them in the dog's diet in order to get the full benefit of Vitamin B, and if a dog is being fed a large quantity of eggs regularly it would be advisable to do this. However, a raw egg given several times a week would be quite in order as the yolk of the egg is rich in Biotin so has a compensating effect.

There are breeders who favour herbalist diets where use is made of such items as honey, parsley, seaweed, garlic, elderberry and raspberry leaf, etc., and I had a friend whose dogs were very healthy on this kind of diet though I have never tried it on my dogs. Most of these diets include in their programme a day of starvation once a week and there may be wisdom in this, but it seems rather hard to say 'No feed to-

Ch. Rollingsea Snow Boots and his daughter Ch. Rollingsea Twotrees
Aurora relaxing after a show

Playtime—and how Bobtails enjoy it!

A game of ball with some rather quaint rules

A sturdy litter of puppies just four weeks old

We may look angelic but really we are dreaming up some new mischief

Introductions are so important! This puppy is making friends with a young donkey

An old favourite obviously approves of the baby

This excellent suit comes from Sweden. It gives protection against wet weather and dirt on the way to a show

Ch. Shepton Dolly Grey, daughter of the late Mr H. A. Tilley's famous pre-war winner Ch. Southridge Roger

The author's Ch. Rollingsea Snow Boots, born 15th May, 1965, winner of 18 Challenge Certificates and 12 times Best of Breed, including Crufts 1969

Mrs M. K. Gibson's Ch. Beckington Tom Tod at Richmond Championship Show 1955 when Best of Breed. Winner of 18 Challenge Certificates

day' to an anxious group of dogs all waiting punctually for their meal, for they all appear to have built-in alarm clocks which tell them exactly when it is time for a feed. It is sure my dogs would all look so hurt and astonished I would not be able to face them.

The choice of vitamins is a wide one, including seaweed powder, various forms of Cod Liver Oil or comprehensive vitamin tablets or powders. One has to find something that suits the dog and then to have faith in that. Some breeders give a course of one type of vitamin and then change to something else, perhaps giving oil in winter time and comprehensive vitamins in the warmer weather, but no matter what you choose to give in the way of vitamins these do help to give that final bloom. The inclusion of some form of oil is excellent for a long coated dog, olive oil, Cod Liver Oil or corn oil are all good, or one of the newer brands of oil advertised as 'containing polyunsaturates which go straight to the skin'. Oil certainly does go to the skin, making it supple and helping the growth and condition of the coat. If one rubs a hand over the coat of a dog that is fed Cod Liver Oil, it is noticeable that quite a strong fishy smell is left on the hand. It is very apparent the way oil will give life and sheen to a dry coat. A point to remember is that oil not only nourishes the skin and coat but it tends to be fattening and it is necessary to keep a close watch on the dog's weight.

The majority of dogs find great pleasure gnawing at a bone and this pastime has two main advantages; one is that the teeth are kept clean and the other is that if a dog gives his attention to gnawing a bone he will be less inclined to chew the table legs or walls or whatever takes its fancy when there is nothing particularly to do and he is bored. Often dogs are not given bones because they are considered harmful and it is true that all splintery bones are unsuitable, but a good solid marrow bone is perfectly safe if given for a period of about fifteen minutes when it is fresh and a little longer when it has been used for a few days. Long sessions of gnaw-

D

ing when the bone is fresh and full of marrow will probably cause the dog to scour, and when a bone has been worked on for a number of sessions, small pieces come off and when swallowed can cause impacted intestines. My own dogs often get a bone to gnaw for a short while after their main meal and this has the effect of keeping their breath sweet and cleaning their teeth.

Another nutritious food is dried fish and this keeps for a long while providing it is stored in an airtight tin. It is obtainable in medium sized pieces and although it can be used to form a main meal I use this mainly as an addition to the diet to give the dog something to make it work hard with its teeth and jaws, much as it would with a bone so that once again this is a titbit and a toothcleaner, also it makes the gastric juices work. As a main meal, it is sufficient to give about three or four pieces of dried fish for an adult bobtail for this swells to about five times the weight, but you feed it dry not soaked.

Of course, it is possible for a dog to survive on very much less and on much different feeding from all that is explained here, and some dogs will not require as much as others, but, if an incorrectly balanced diet is given, or only a little of the least expensive food, then it is more than likely that what is saved on the feeding bills will be spent in pills and potients at the chemist or on veterinary advice for attention to the troubles that would not have occurred had the dog been properly fed. There are so many varieties of dog foods on the market today and almost as many methods of feeding and being the case, if six breeders were asked for a diet sheet, they may well come up with six different reliable instructions, but basically they will contain protein, carbohydrates and vitamins, whichever way they choose to feed them.

If the dog's food is served in a lightweight dish, it is likely to be tipped over very easily, therefore one of the most serviceable types of dish to use is a good heavy quality enamel pie dish which is easy to clean and should be picked up and washed after each meal and put away until the next feed.

Feeding will be the same for one dog living in the house or for each of several dogs in kennels, though with the latter there is the advantage that the owner can buy in larger quantities at a keener price, getting sacks of dog biscuit meal or complete feed pellets and, with any luck, a consignment of meat or tripe from the local slaughter house. All the dry foods should be kept in a cool dry place and can be stored in plastic bins with airtight lids. Meat also must be hygenically stored, preferably in a refrigerator.

5

EXERCISE AND KENNEL
ROUTINE

It is unlikely that anyone will aspire to keeping a great
number of Old English Sheepdogs as the coat requires more
than average attention and so makes heavy demands on
one's time – a commodity most of us have in short supply –
therefore the kennel routine we will consider will be relating
to about six adults and an occasional litter of puppies. Unless
you have no other work to do or you have help of some kind
such as a kennel maid, you will find it impossible to do justice
to more than six or seven bobtails, or even less.

The first task in the morning is to let all the dogs out in
their runs, unless you want them to soil their kennels, and
leave them in their runs if it is fine, whilst you have breakfast
and until you are ready to see to them again.

When two young dogs are kennelled together, they exercise
each other by playing and running about together. Whereas
one dog on its own will lie down or sit waiting for something
to happen, hoping someone will come and rescue him soon,
two young dogs enjoy each other's company and seem to
think of no end of wickedness, like digging holes in the
ground or running about with any object they can find such
as a piece of stick, teasing their companion into a game. In-
evitably they rag out a great deal of each other's coat, but
this does not matter too much unless you wish to show them.
It seems a pity not to let them have as much natural enjoyment as possible, but when wanting to show them it is wise
to kennel a young dog with an older sedate animal who will
not play wild games or rag about.

In addition to the exercise two dogs will get from playing if they are kennelled together, they benefit from regular exercise. I am a great believer in regular daily walks and all my dogs go out in the morning and again in the late afternoon, either in the lanes for road exercise or for a gallop in the fields and by doing this, I find they rarely soil their runs. Road exercise is excellent for developing muscles and keeping feet in good shape, whilst free exercise will stretch their legs and generally develop the muscles, apart from being full of interest to the dogs. In summer time when all the dogs spend more time out in their runs, it does not matter if they do not go very far but exercise should be regular and the dogs soon know when it is time for their outing and eagerly look forward to it. The distance they ought to go depends very much on what kind of life they lead and exactly how much freedom is given them during the remainder of the day.

At some time each day each of our dogs is allowed to come in the house with us for a while, that is once it has become a settled inmate of the kennel, and during this time it is possible to make sure it is house trained. It is far more pleasant to spend the time house training the dogs and exercising them, rather than not taking them out of their runs or kennels and having to spend an equivalent amount of time cleaning out houses and clearing up soiled runs.

It is most important to keep the runs clean either by exercising the dogs outside away from the run or by regular clearing up of the runs. If neglected, the run would get unpleasant and would smell and attract flies and also be liable to get infected by bacteria which is not easy to eliminate. Apart from that, just occasionally one gets a dog with the unpleasant habit of eating its own excreta or that of another dog. It is difficult to know what causes this habit but it is very important to clean up the run so that this can be avoided. Normally once the habit is broken the dog appears to forget all about doing such a thing.

Another advantage of regular outings, is that, whilst a dog

is walking along the road, he can be taught to walk properly on a loose lead and a relationship develops which is quite impossible to attain by brief visits to the kennels; an understanding which is invaluable when one is to show the dog, for you know so well how he reacts to different circumstances and you can show together as a team.

When there are young puppies to attend to, the walking sessions will have to fit in, either earlier or later, to suit the puppy routine which must be fairly punctual.

Grooming will fit in the programme when it is most convenient and to get each dog groomed twice a week it will be necessary to groom one or two dogs each day. The attention you give the dog whilst grooming and whilst walking will be invaluable in other ways, for one thing during these times there will be opportunity to notice the slightest change in his behaviour, any sign at all of being off colour such as weeping eyes, waxy ears, sore places, dry skin or the presence of parasites. If you discover something wrong you can give immediate attention before the trouble gets worse.

Apart from the physical benefit derived from being exercised, the dog finds this a break in the monotony of kennel life. A family dog living in the house has events happening all the time to gain his attention, but unless you think out ways of diverting a kennel dog, it could get very bored even with a companion, though a companion does help the situation enormously. Obedience training, which helps to exercise the dog's mind, is especially important for the bobtail being a working dog, and in short sessions will prove an enjoyable diversion. I have never been to obedience classes, although these must be excellent for getting a dog used to the presence of other dogs as well as training them to be obedient, but I have my own method of simple training and this usually proves enjoyable as well as instructive. Other welcome breaks in kennel life include bone chewing and the grooming session.

When there is an errand to be done in the car (automobile)

I take one or two of the dogs with me. This not only breaks the monotony but accustoms them to car travel and they learn to behave and not jump about in the car, particularly if a youngster goes for a drive with an adult dog that is an experienced traveller. When dogs are travelling in a car particularly of the Estate variety they like a piece of rubber backed carpeting or similar non-skid covering as a surface to lie on to stop them sliding about with the movement of the car. They also require ventilation especially when the car is parked because heat builds up very rapidly in a stationary car and in a short time on a sunny day the bakingly hot conditions cause great suffering to a dog and in some cases death. It is quite surprising that a tremendous number of people, including many dog owners, do not realise the danger of leaving dogs in a car without sufficient ventilation and it does not occur to them to park in a shady place. Nowadays it is possible to buy an expanding guard which is fixed along the top of the car window and gives several inches of ventilation, giving the dog the benefit of fresh air but preventing his escape by jumping out of the window. Even so it is important to park the car in the shade if it is to be left for any length of time or for a short time on a hot day.

Occasionally one gets a dog that will insist on jumping over into the front seat or one that fidgets unduly during the journey and in this case it is best to buy a dog guard which, when erected, will keep the dog in its own part of the car. Estate cars are getting increasingly popular as the best type of car if any amount of travelling is to be done with dogs, as, for instance, travelling to shows, especially with a large dog like the bobtail.

If a puppy is taken short journeys from quite a young age, it should get accustomed to car travel, but some adult dogs still get travel sick and in this case your Veterinary Surgeon can prescribe a travel pill to stop the sickness. It is very rare to get a dog that cannot eventually be cured of travel sickness but it can happen. Most dogs get confidence once they

Some breeds are easy to spot on the road to a Dog Show...

have done one or two journeys without being sick and then providing the driving is fairly steady they should not have any more trouble. Some young puppies are never sick and travel happily in a car from an early age, but if you have a puppy who is sick, keep taking him in the car and sit him on a newspaper to absorb the dribble and persevere by taking him daily, if possible, until he has overcome his fear of the car in motion. Never go long, tedious journeys with a puppy that is a poor traveller but it is advisable to go short journeys, about 2 or 3 miles, to begin with in order to improve matters. It is a matter of gaining confidence and overcoming the fear of car travel and by going these very short trips, which should be undertaken before feeding the puppy, it is likely it will be home again safely before being sick. If this is repeated a number of times successfully gradually the journeys can be lengthened.

We had one particularly bad traveller in spite of taking her in the car when she was a very small puppy and I remember writing reports of her progress to my daughter at school. To begin with it was impossible to go 2 miles without sickness, but in a short while the report was '. . . she did 23 miles per sick . . .' and then we took the puppy to a show and this involved a long journey so she was given a travel pill. The result was that she showed no sign of feeling sick and thereafter could travel without any thought of being sick and without ever taking another travel pill. This is one of a number of puppies I have cured by taking them very short successful journeys in their early days and I am sure that in the majority of cases it is just a matter of overcoming their nerves.

If you think out a routine to suit your own particular way of life and one that gives the dogs plenty of interest, you will have happy, alert and intelligent animals. Dogs that are left for hours on end in a kennel and run cannot get sufficient exercise of brain or limbs and some become inveterate barkers, some become dull and stodgey and others become chewers, chewing the kennel door and window frame or anything they can.

Oddly enough I own a youngster who still does a great amount of chewing and to such an extent that the kennel doorway and the door have had to be repaired and edged with metal strips; and this is not because of boredom because he has plenty of variety in his life. I think he is an exception and must just like the taste of wood!

Cleaning the kennels and putting clean bedding will have to be done regularly for it will soon become dusty, but in good fine weather it will, of course, last a little longer than when the weather is wet and mud is brought in on the dog's feet to dry off. Another regular part of the routine is to fill the buckets in the kennels with fresh water.

After the evening feed, which is the main meal for the dogs, they will be housed for the night, except in long summer days when they can go in and out as they please until about 10 o'clock at night. When it is dark, I like to think my dogs are safely housed in their kennels, well fed, well exercised and comfortable. It is not unusual for dogs to be kennelled from about 5 o'clock when it is dark in winter time, until next morning, but I always let my dogs out in their run before going to bed myself about 10 or 11 o'clock at night. They go out quickly, knowing exactly the purpose of this brief run, and rush back to their beds waiting for the small biscuit I give them all as a titbit before going to bed for the night.

Having established a routine to fit in with your domestic arrangements, it will be quite simple to look after your dogs, but if someone who is not used to them offers to look after them for you to go away for a few days, it is quite extraordinary how difficult it is to explain to them in a short time all the details of your daily round.

6

THE COAT AND GROOMING

If you read carefully the requirements for the coat and its colour in the Breed Standard, you will realise that this demands a great deal and that it is necessary to breed for sound animals which possess as near as possible the coat required. That is to say, it is essential in the first place to 'breed' for a good coat.

The colour is very important and brown, sable or fawn are considered objectionable. One sees dogs of a variety of shades from pigeon blue to dark grey and providing they are not tinged with brown, they are acceptable; some shades being more attractive and popular than others. If a dog's coat is rather too pale – a washed out kind of colour – it is wise to mate the dog to one having a deeper shade to improve coat colour. A very dark coloured dog should mate with a lighter shade for the same reason. So that colour is something we can improve by careful breeding though it will take more than one generation to establish coats of an improved shade.

Some coats appear a true blue but turn colour easily to acquire a brownish tinge. It can happen if the dog is exposed to too much sunshine and I have known this to happen to a dog belonging to a lady living on the coast, where there was supposedly too much salt atmosphere. When the lady became ill, the dog was shut in the house practically all day for several weeks and its coat looked beautiful and clear of any brown for the first time for some years. Although exposure to the sun and salt atmosphere can therefore alter the coat colour, it would seem to be wrong to keep dogs shut in simply to preserve coat colour as they should live a normal life. Sometimes the coat appears a poor colour because the undercoat has not been sufficiently groomed, for the dead undercoat will turn brown.

A harsh texture is required and whilst this is inherited, the texture can be greatly influenced by environment. The dog should be housed where it is not too warm; it should be comfortable and not icy cold, but having a heavy jacket to withstand the rigours of the climate, a bobtail can be comfortable housed in a temperature that would be much too low for a smooth coated animal. House the dog where it is well ventilated and cool, never damp and draughty, and nature will see that the coat responds. I have noticed that dogs which are housed indoors, particularly where there is central heating, tend to become soft coated. The atmosphere is warm and comfortable for humans but far too warm for heavily coated dogs. On the other hand, two of my puppies were exported to Alaska and there, in the extreme cold, they grew very heavy harsh coats indeed to withstand the climate.

When considering the harshness of the coat, this refers to the top coat, for the bobtail carries a double coat, a harsh top coat and a soft wool undercoat which is waterproof. It is the undercoat that is first to mat if neglected. Some bobtails carry to much undercoat and insufficient top coat and this gives a woolly effect and is a very difficult coat to keep free of mats. More rarely there are bobtails with plenty of top coat and very little undercoat and this is an easy type of coat to groom but never looks quite right as there must be sufficient of the undercoat to give body to the whole effect and to stand the top coat up, but if it lacks undercoat the result can look a bit lank.

Another requirement is a profuse coat and this will depend on whether the particular dog is predisposed to grow a profuse coat, but again this can be greatly influenced by the kind of feeding. An adequate, balanced diet is required which includes a little oil, particularly in winter time, as suggested in the chapter on feeding, and it is easy to imagine the effect oil has on the coat.

I note the American Breed Standard states 'Profuse but not so excessive as to give the impression of the dog being over fat.' That is a good point, for one sometimes comes across dogs with a coat which is so profuse that it completely spoils the dog's outline. One can comb out an excessive coat around the neck and shoulders and generally improve the shape of the dog when grooming by reducing the coat where necessary, for a very profuse coat left to its own devices will obliterate the good points of a well shaped dog and give the impression of fatness.

Another way the dog's outline gets lost is when there is a long, soft coat which is rather straight and without the correct 'break'. A coat with the correct 'break' is one that has the correct kink or wave to make it a shaggy coat. There is a type of coat with the correct break which is harsh and of reasonable length, not long and flowing, which is very fitting for a working dog and this never hides the outline.

The shagginess of the coat is something it has or has not; some coats are too straight and flat looking and a few are a shade too curly, but the ideal is somewhere between the two and if it is harsh and a good colour as well as shaggy, then it is the ideal coat.

The grooming kit required to cope with a bobtail's coat must include a suitable brush, one of whalebone with a handle and with the bristles well spaced so that it can get into the coat. Close set bristles do not penetrate a dense coat. All the brushing necessary can be done with this type of brush, but some people like a brush of this type for the main part of the coat and then use a cushioned brush with bristles even more widely set to brush up the leg featherings and for the finishing touches. Another requirement is a steel comb and there are two types which are most popular; one measuring 5 in. long with strong round teeth set $\frac{1}{6}$ in. apart and 2 in. long, or one measuring 7 in. long with 1 in. round teeth set ⅛ in. apart.

Other items in the grooming kit will be a pair of moderate-sized straight scissors, a pair of thinning scissors and a pair of small, curved scissors, a small quantity of cotton wool, canker powder, container of chalk powder for general cleansing of the white parts and a Zepto stick, which is not a veterinary product but is sold at any chemist for human use for scaling any accumulations of tartar off the teeth.

Most bobtails love to be groomed as they enjoy the attention lavished on them and providing any mats are attacked with care and gentleness, they behave really well for the grooming sessions. Even so, it is wise to begin when a puppy is young, say six or seven weeks, by making it keep still whilst it is brushed for a short while as this will prepare it for regular grooming sessions later on; also a little gentle brushing even at such a tender age will serve to rid the coat of any bits of straw or shavings or dirt picked up when playing in the run.

From an early age, teach the puppy to stand on a table to be groomed as this saves a lot of back-ache from bending down to their level to brush. The table should not be too high and it must be firm as no dog likes a wobbly surface. An old fashioned wooden table makes a good solid grooming table. Once a dog is big enough to jump up on the table, it will be only too thrilled to do so and will lie there waiting for attention. It is easier to groom an adult lying down on the table.

The appearance of pale blue-grey hairs on the hocks or down over the puppy's shoulders will herald the beginning of the second coat and as it is best to help this to come through as quickly as possible, the daily gentle brushing will have to become a brushing and combing session. Gradually the baby coat will begin to shed and will come away in the comb and when this is happening there can be free use of the comb after brushing in order to remove all dead hair which, if left, will be quick to mat. The first appearance of the second coat can be as early as eight weeks or as late as eight months, but the average is at three to four months and it will take several months to change completely. This means that from the time the puppy coat loosens until the second coat is mostly through it is wise to give a brisk brushing followed by free use of the comb.

When the dog has lost the majority of its puppy coat it is important to restrict the free use of the comb except around the neck and ears and down over the shoulders and at the rear. Every hair counts on the head, also on the rump and legs and all coat on these parts must be cherished but at the same time be kept free of mats. If a mat is beginning to form on any of these parts, it may be quite easily teased out with your fingers, if not, hold the matted piece of hair between finger and thumb of one hand and, holding the comb in the other hand, use only the point of the comb as in Fig. 5 to tease the hair apart; sometimes it is easier to finish the job with fingers only, but on no account use the comb to drag through the mat taking a clump of hair in its wake.

At somewhere between 12 and 18 months the coat will probably be very light in colour and gradually it will settle to the final adult coat with the shade darkening.

Fig. 5 Teasing out matted hair

There are various methods for dealing with the coat of an adult bobtail; it can get a little attention each day or a reasonable going over twice a week or a long session once a week. Choosing from these, I advise the two sessions a week unless it is a very difficult and woolly coat in which case I would prefer to groom daily to keep ahead of the knots. Giving a long session once a week is likely to be tiring for the dog and also for the one who is grooming and patience may get a little frayed on both sides.

Some years ago, my husband came across an elderly couple who had a bobtail and when he first saw the dog it was about two years old and a mass of knots. He persuaded them to let me call and see if I could help them groom the dog, which could not be referred to as neglected for it was their pride and joy. They spoiled him, over-fed him and let him lead them a rare old dance, and they appeared to believe they looked after Bob perfectly. The lady assured me she spent two hours every day brushing him and, if so, all her energy was directed on a ridge just down the middle of his back for that part was not matted in the least; other than that one ridge it was impossible to get the comb to penetrate for it was a solid felt mat all over. I was about to examine his ears but she told me that he did not like his ears touched, or his toes or, it seemed, anywhere on him except the ridge down the centre of his back. She confided that sometimes, when he was asleep, she crept up and tried to groom some of the areas that he did not approve of being groomed, but with little success. The hardest part of our task was convincing this couple that the dog was uncomfortable and would be improved if he had a properly groomed coat, and imagine what parasites might be harboured in that felt. Ultimately they agreed to take him to the Veterinary Surgeon who could sedate him whilst they removed his fleece. Sadly enough, in a few short months after the shearing his coat was thickening up again and I would make a guess it was because he dared them to touch him with a brush and comb!

Of course this dog was thoroughly spoiled and mishandled and is an exception to the vast majority who love to be groomed. When grooming a normal adult bobtail we expect it to jump up on the grooming table and lie down for attention.

For every day grooming, begin with the head and first clean away any accumulation of dirt from the corners of the eyes as, if these are left, they could cause soreness in time. A dog cannot clean its own eyes but if the dirt is left to accumulate, he may try to rid himself of this by rubbing against objects or rubbing his face along the carpet. Occasionally a bobtail gets a loose hair in the eye and you may be able to remove this by getting it between your fingers; if not, it is quite easy as a rule to secure one end of the hair with a small dampened piece of cotton wool.

Attending to the head coat, search for any mats of hair and separate them by teasing them apart as already explained, then brush first one side of the head and then the other with an upward stroke, leaving the hair to settle like a halo. If the fall (hair immediately over the eyes) is not very long brush it down towards the nose, but in many adults with a long, thick fall of hair, it would cover the nose and spoil the outline of the head, so if it is long brush the fall back and away from the face, then put one hand over the muzzle close by the eyes and with the other hand brush the hair forward over your hand. This accentuates the stop (the rise to the forehead at the base of the muzzle) und will improve the outline of the foreface.

When grooming for show purposes, the head coat is left falling over the eyes and is brushed as described, but for everyday purposes it is wise to tie the hair up, in order that the dog may see properly once it has grown a heavy fall of hair. Originally the fall of hair was not nearly so long or so thick and the bobtail's long eyelashes kept it out of the eyes and served to shade the eyes from the glare of the sun or snow so that the dog could see well when working with

E

sheep in all conditions. With the thick fall of hair on many modern bobtails they really cannot see properly and tend to bump into objects unless the hair is tied up. One of the neatest ways to do this is to brush the hair immediately over the eyes upward and gather a tuft into your hand; bend the tuft over and then place a small elastic band around the middle of the doubled tuft and twist the band around once or twice more to make it firm. This is shown in Fig. 6.

FIG. 6 A neat method of tying up hair over the eyes

There are nearly always little patches where the hair is beginning to mat below and behind the ears, also on the ear flaps and these need attention.

When grooming the neck and shoulders, free use can be made of the comb, thus pulling out a certain amount of coat which is necessary to keep the look of elegance of a good neck. If the coat is allowed to thicken on the neck and shoulders the dog appears to be wide at the front and short-necked. Thinning out the coat by combing not only helps to show off the neckline but will show a good pair of shoulders to advantage. It is not possible to have really good shoulders on a dog that is overweight because the fat will prise the shoulder blades apart and no amount of careful grooming can rectify this; the dog would be described as being 'loaded at the shoulders' and slimming is necessary.

Around the neck and shoulder region, the feet, and at the rear of the dog are areas which require a certain amount of extra combing, rasping or even delicately performed attention with the scissors to keep sleek neck and shoulders, neat feet and to present the body looking as short as possible. Also ear tassels require rasping to shorten, and other than these aids to shaping the Old English Sheepdog is presented naturally.

Get the dog lying on his side and part the hair in lines or sections, teasing out any mats, then give the whole side a brisk brushing. Special attention is necessary to the underneath of the dog and behind the forelegs and in front of the hindlegs close to the body as the friction when the dog is in action causes a certain amount of matting. Once again use your fingers for any mats and where necessary use the point of the comb to separate them, never tug and never use the width of the comb in undoing mats as this is painful for the dog and takes out too much coat.

When one side is finished, turn the dog over and repeat the process on the other side. Lastly stand the dog up on the ground and make sure there are no knots on the back, then brush briskly all over in the directions indicated in Fig. 7.

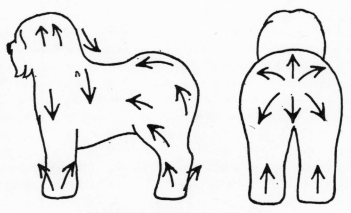

Fig. 7 Directions for brushing coat

It is not a good thing to make a habit of bathing a bobtail, even though it should be kept clean, as this softens the coat. It is better to give regular grooming sessions, and brushing will rid the coat of dried mud or dust of any kind. The use of a chamois leather for drying a dog on a wet day will also do much to keep the coat clean. Once the coat has been bathed, the natural oil is washed out to a great extent and this renders the coat more liable to pick up dirt than before. A coat with all its natural oil is much easier to keep clean. There are times such as after a long dry spell of summer weather, when it is wise to freshen the coat with an all over bath, but normally there is no need to do this and it is only the white parts that might improve with a bit of shampoo, though a little cleaning chalk used during the grooming session occasionally, should do all that is required to keep the white sparkling.

In my early days of showing a bobtail, about 20 years ago, I was told that the use of scissors on a bobtail was frowned upon and that one way to get the feet looking neatly rounded was to singe away the excess hair with a lighted taper – this to be done about two weeks before a show, although I never practised this method myself. The rear trimming was done by finger and thumb plucking out or shortening some of the coat and the same method was used for shortening the ear tassels. I found I could trim feet very delicately with a pair of scissors and they did not look as if they had been cut in any way and I continue to use the same method today. Get the dog lying down with forelegs stretched in front and, doing one foot at a time, brush back away from the foot all but the first thin layer of hair above the toes and if the line is jagged, shape it to be round by using first the thinning scissors and finishing off with the straight scissors. If there are any large spiky pieces of hair spoiling the line, you can improve matters by using the thinning scissors, but there will be a feathery line which needs attention with the straight scissors to get a perfect round, just covering the nails. Next, bring down another thin layer of hair and repeat the procedure, always just covering the nails, and do this each time bringing down a thin layer until all the hair has been checked. Comb the hair down into position and check for any hairs that have been missed.

Having attended to the front feet turn your attention to the hind feet, and with the dog standing trim the front of each hind foot as for the front feet. You can also use thinning scissors for trimming any excess feathering at the back of the hind feet; that is, if the feathering is trailing along the ground. Comb out after using the thinning scissors for this and then, with the straight scissors, feather trim any pieces remaining in excess.

The top of all feet will now have received attention and it is necessary to concentrate on the underneath of the feet by making the dog lie down and, with the little curved scissors, remove most of the hair from between the pads. This is done to stop the thick growth of hair picking up mud and small stones and congealing to form a hard knot between the pads as it will cause soreness which can get quite acute. Also it is to stop great bunches of hair spreading a neat foot and, apart from these reasons, the dog will bring far less mess into the house if the feet are neatly trimmed. The feet will require trimming at intervals of four to six weeks according to the rate of growth of the hair.

A word about nails before we dismiss the feet. These should be as short as possible without wearing down to the quick and the ideal way is to walk the dog on rough roads, but if this is not possible then the area of rough concrete suggested as part of a kennel run should produce the desired result. A dog with long nails cannot possibly move well.

During the regular grooming session examine the dog's ears inside the flap; some dogs have remarkably clean ears and others, particularly whilst they are young, get a brown waxy discharge. From three months onwards, watch the ears for excessive wax as you will very often find a youngster has dead hair and wax down in the ear. To attend to this, shake a little canker powder onto a piece of cotton wool, using the powder as a little dusting powder and not filling the ear, and gently wipe the ear flap and the part of the ear that is visible. Remove any brown waxy deposit with care as the ear is most sensitive and rough handling can do more harm than good. Tweak out any hair from the centre of the ear and, if there are any large pieces of wax deep down, you may be able to get these by working them up gently with a piece of cotton wool. Never use anything hard like an orange stick in the ear. If you cannot get the wax out with cotton wool, it may be necessary to buy some ear drops and use them as directed to loosen the wax. An ear which is neglected can get very sore and inflamed and may lead to canker.

There should be regular inspection of the dog's teeth and if marrow bones are given to the dog from time to time and dried fish included in the diet, it is unlikely that there will be much tartar accumulating. There is practically always a small deposit of tartar at the neck of the canine teeth, presumably bone chewing does not quite reach this; also some dogs keep very clean teeth all their life and others get tartar on all the teeth very quickly. To scale off tartar, use a Zepto stock, which is formed rather like a pencil and has a pointed end. It contains pumice and is very easy to use for cleaning the dog's teeth. Excessive use of this stick would cause damage to the enamel of the teeth, but if used carefully every month or two is quite safe.

To get the best out of a bobtail's body shape and accentuate a short, square body, there will be a great improvement if any excessive overhang of coat is removed from the rear end. Although finger and thumb plucking was the old way to trim this, very few people rely on this method nowadays. It is possible to use scissors discreetly to trim the rear. Stand the dog on the floor, with his rear towards you and, making the tail stump as a marker, brush the hair above the stump forward over his body and the hair below it down over his legs. Taking a small clump of hair at the centre of the stump, trim it with the thinning scissors, then comb it out, gathering the remaining hair and, with the straight scissors feather trim to leave about ¾ in. of hair on the stump. Next, bring down a thin layer of hair from just above the stump and close the thinning scissors on it, comb out and then feather trim to make it lie just level with the hair on the stump. Taking a thin layer at a time, do this until there is no overhang of coat above the stump. Using the thinning scissors, thin the coat below the tail stump and on either side, so that when it is combed in each direction away from the tail stump, it will lie neatly and give a squareness which would not have been so evident before. You should brush the coat above the tail marker up and over the rear and by brushing out on either side of the tail stump, it will give a look of width.

There is one other item of trimming which is sometimes necessary and that is the tassels on the ears. When you have groomed the dog, sit him facing you and try to assess whether the ears look too long in proportion to the head, very often the effect is greatly improved by combing or plucking out a little of the tassel and with finger and thumb, shortening the tassels a little. This should be done delicately and never drastically or it will look terrible. The best way is to do a very little and leave it for a day or so and if it is evident that a little more should come off you can always have a second attempt, but if you overdo things in the first instance, it is not possible to rectify the matter.

7

SHOWING

The mention of showing a dog will most likely conjure up a picture of someone having to work very hard grooming a dog for that very important occasion known as a dog show, especially when the dog is an Old English Sheepdog, but whilst a well groomed dog is required, that is only one aspect of the situation.

To begin with one has to find out what dog shows there are, the various types of shows, which is most suitable to make an entry and where and when they are being held. The types of shows in England are as follows :

Shows held under Kennel Club licence, including:

Limited Shows. These are unbenched shows limited to members of the club or society holding the show or exhibitors have to come from a limited area. Dogs that have won any award counting towards the title of Champion are not eligible.

Open Shows. These can be benched provided more than 60 classes have been scheduled, otherwise they are unbenched. They are open to all dogs from any part of the country. Breeds that are numerically strong often have several classes scheduled, but unusual breeds have to compete in Variety classes. Bobtails used rarely to have classes in the past, but nowadays some Open shows include one or two classes for Old English Sheepdogs and sometimes an Open show puts on a classification of four to six classes.

Championship Shows. A great variety of breeds are

scheduled at these shows with classification according to the numerical strength of the breed. In the majority of breeds Challenge Certificates are offered, that is a Challenge Certificate for the best dog and a Challenge Certificate for the best bitch in a breed. In order to gain the title of Champion, it is necessary for a dog to win three Challenge Certificates under three different Judges at Championship shows where Challenge Certificates are allotted to the breed.

Other types of shows:

Sanction Shows. These are unbenched shows where no dog is eligible over Post Graduate grade and they are run for the benefit of bona fide members of a Club.

Exemption Shows. The word exemption refers to the fact that the dogs do not necessarily have to be registered at the Kennel Club and are therefore exempt from Kennel Club registration. Only four classes for pedigree dogs are permitted and the remainder of the schedule is comprised of Novelty classes and there can be obedience classes, but these must differ from those set out in Kennel Club rules and regulations. Often these shows are run in conjunction with other functions such as a fete, to raise money for charity. Wins at exemption shows do not count when assessing wins in connection with entry at Kennel Club licence shows. Exemption shows with their garden party atmosphere are enjoyable and can be useful for taking a dog to gain experience of being handled, but are not taken too seriously.

There are dog matches held under Kennel Club rules. A club may have as many as one a month and these have an informal atmosphere and can be useful for getting a dog used to being handled and behaving with other dogs.

Sanction shows and Limited shows provide a useful training ground for a youngster, for a dog must be schooled to walk on a loose lead and to stand quietly to be looked at and examined by the judge, also to stand and look alert whilst in the show ring. After outings of this kind a puppy should be ready to go to classes at an Open or Championship show where there are classes for the breed. It is better to assess the dog by comparing with a class of the same breed and classification.

An Old English Sheepdog puppy does not mature quickly as a rule and a puppy of six or seven months will look very much the baby of the class.

The Kennel Club rules in England allow for scheduling an Open class at Championship shows, which is open to all dogs and this includes Champions, whereas in America once a dog has gained its title of Champion, it cannot enter except in the Champion class and therefore is removed from competing in the class with up and coming dogs. With the British system the Champions can go on indefinitely gaining Challenge Certificates if they wish, and new dogs have to beat them to gain a title. If there are one or two star dogs about, it takes a while to do this. Whether it is good to have a dog gaining a great number of Challenge Certificates is one of the questions which comes up for discussion from time to time, for it is a very debatable subject. The title of Champion in America is worked on a points system, with three to five for major wins, and to gain the title of Champion a total of fifteen points is necessary.

Before entering a show a dog should be registered at the Kennel Club and, if it has changed hands, the transfer form should be completed and sent to the Kennel Club. Normally a dog does not have to have any qualification other than the registration at the Kennel Club in order to enter a Kennel Club licence show, but Cruft's Dog Show, held early in February each year, is an exception. For Cruft's Dog Show 1967 a qualifying system was put in operation and dogs had to qualify during the previous year. Basically under this system Champions were eligible, or dogs which won a Challenge Certificate or a first, second or third prize in a breed class at a Championship show (whether there were Kennel Club Challenge Certificates for the breed or not) between

1st January and 31 December of the previous year. This
system was considered a success, achieving its aim to get a
high standard of quality for the dogs exhibited at Cruft's,
but after a few years it seemed that there was room for improvement in order to get the best of young stock as well as
the best of mature stock. To this end Cruft's Show Committee
decided in April 1972 to submit new qualifying rules for the
1973 Cruft's Dog Show.

For the main requirements, once again Champions would
be eligible and dogs winning a Challenge Certificate under
Kennel Club rules, or winning the following prizes at Championship Shows where Challenge Certificates were offered for
the breed between 1st January and 31st December in the
previous year :

First or second in puppy class
First or second in junior class
First in novice class
First in post graduate class
First or second in limit class
First, second or third in open class

The only other show to request a qualification, since its
1971 show, is Blackpool Championship Show. In this case
the main requirement is that a dog must have won a Challenge Certificate or a first, second or third prize at a Championship or Open show at any time, in a breed class.

There are two weekly dog papers, *Our Dogs* and *Dog
World*, which come out on Friday and they give announce-
ments of forthcoming shows so that you can discover the
ones in your area. All you have to do is to write to the
Secretary of the show for a schedule and then be sure to get
your entry in before the closing date because this is a rule
very strictly kept.

After a show a judge writes a report of the placings, with
comments, about the winning dogs, and this appears in the
dog press. By reading some of these you may get an idea
of what the various judges ask of a dog and learn from the

Some judges go for the larger type...

write-ups the faults and virtues which they consider worthy of mention.

Having decided on a suitable show for bringing out your dog or puppy, you will have to try and see he is on top form and, if you have been feeding him well and giving regular exercise, it is to be hoped he will not be too fat or too lean and that he is well muscled. It will be necessary to concentrate on practice of ringcraft, with particular emphasis on getting him to stand still whilst he is examined and to walk on a loose lead. Find out what you can do to help him to look alert whilst in the ring; maybe a titbit in your hand will do this. A natural showman will look interested and alert without your help and this is worth a great deal.

When preparing a dog for show, it must be groomed thoroughly in readiness. About two weeks before the show all trimming can be done, neatening the ears, neck, shoulders and rear, also the feet. Be sure to check that ears and teeth are properly clean.

Never present a dog to the judge in a dirty or partly prepared state. Usually regular brushing and the occasional use of a coat dressing will keep it clean. The white parts will need washing if they are very dirty, but if they just need freshening up this can be done with a little cleansing powder. If the body coat is dirty enough to warrant a bath, this should be done at least a week before the show as bathing softens the coat and there must be time for the coat to harshen up again before the show. The white parts can be bathed a day or two before showing.

Thoroughly groom the whole of the dog's coat about two or three days before the show and then leave it to body up again ready to be groomed out on the day of the show.

For a benched show one needs a chain to fasten the dog on the bench, a rug for him to lie on and the show bag containing schedule and pass to the show, brush, comb, cleansing powder, a towel, show lead, drinking bowl and container of water and dog's feed if you are to be away over night. He will, of course, be taken to the show on a collar and lead.

Regarding the collar, the best kind for a bobtail is a round leather one as the normal flat collars tend to rub away the coat and flatten it down. Obviously a strongly made collar is necessary as a bobtail is strong if it pulls. The lead also must be strong and I advise a heavy trigger clip as being the safest. Before trigger clips were available, I used a scissor clip and had the fright of a youngster giving a sudden pull and getting free in London traffc. Also the spring type clip let me down when one young dog was free and I had another on a lead; he pulled suddenly and the spring broke and both dogs were playing and running madly on a cliff where there was a sheer drop below into the sea. After that I fixed at least two clips on all my leads until strong trigger clips came on the market.

Always leave plenty of time to get to a show, for traffic is sometimes conjested particularly near the show ground and will slow you up. The dog will take his mood from you; if you are nervous or late and in a hurry with patience running short, it will not settle to be the calm showman you are hoping to produce.

The final grooming will be done on the day when you arrive at the show and this should be done placidly and not in a tremendous hurry and be sure you groom in a place set aside for this purpose if there is one; never fling hair and chalk about with gay abandon. For the reputation of the breed, please carry a plastic bag and put all combings and rubbish in this to take home for disposal.

The dog's whiskers can be cleaned by dampening them and then rubbing them with a rough towel and then place the towel either side of the whiskers and sprinkle a little cleansing powder so that the two parts of the towel can be rubbed against each other with whiskers and powder between them. This works wonders with discoloured whiskers and if left for an hour or so after this treatment, they are then ready to comb out and the effect is very good.

It is very important that a dog enjoys show days, particularly his first shows, and it does not matter so much whether he wins or looses although it is always pleasant to be in the cards, but if the first few shows are enjoyable your dog will look forward to these jaunts which he will look on as a journey in the car and a day spent happily in your company with titbits given when you eat your lunch. For the first few shows never enter more than two classes, as the best of young dogs tend to get bored and I have seen more than one promising dog spoiled by being entered in six or seven classes at an Open show where they have Variety classes to go through. In order to do well with the dog he must not be allowed to get bored or over-tired and fed up because you have left him alone on his bench for a long time.

He must enjoy the outings and then he will be in a mood to look like a showman and give of his best. There are the exceptions, the dogs that never enjoy a day's showing no matter how hard you try to make it a specially pleasant day, but usually in time they at least come to accept the routine. One particularly fine dog of mine was always very bored with the routine no matter what I did and one day whilst we were lining up and waiting for our turn for the judge's examination, he rolled on his back in the ring! It was so unexpected that he was down before I realised what he was doing, but after that I decided to keep him at home and find a kennel mate who did possess that very valuable asset of showmanship.

If a puppy is a good showman and is doing well at his early shows, it is interesting to try and gain his Junior Warrant. For this one has to gain 25 points at Open and Championship shows before he is eighteen months old. Three points for a first and Championship level and one point for a first at Open, in a breed class. Variety class wins do not count.

The photographs of Champions in this book show the position a dog is expected to adopt when standing in the show ring. The judge will be looking for a dog that is typical of the breed, a sound dog, well presented and well enough behaved for it to be seen standing still and for movement to be assessed as it walks in a straight line on a loose lead. He will also be looking for that bit of extra quality, sparkle and showmanship that helps to get a dog to the top.

If you are ever told that you have to be known, or have to be in the breed for years, before being recognised, do not believe it. If you have a good dog and you do your best to handle and present it well, you will get to the top. There is a certain amount of luck as to how many really first class dogs are competing against you – sometimes you are showing the star in poorer company and at other times the competition is very hot. Whatever the decision of the judge at each show, be sure to receive the placing sportingly; if you do not agree and think your dog should have been placed higher, remember there is always another show and another judge; go and seek another opinion.

If it is your aim to own just one dog and you want to show, then you will get a great amount of fun and interest and make a number of very good friends among the Old English Sheepdog fraternity. If you wish to breed and you want to encourage a demand for your puppies so that you can assess the enquiries and choose the ones that would give a good home to each puppy, then it is *necessary* for you to show your stock in order that you get known. If you have a good dog, well reared and well presented which is seen to have a good temperament and which does some winning for you, it will be noticed by both the public and the breeders.

Mr. and Mrs I. Morrison's Ch. Wrightway Blue Mantle, born 18th May, 1966, winner of 10 Challenge Certificates and 8 times Best of Breed

Mr J. D. Featherstone's Ch. Shepton Pick of the Bunch, winner of 7 Challenge Certificates and 5 times Best of Breed, including Crufts 1971

A litter of young puppies at the feeder described in Chapter 9

American Ch. Twotrees Chrysanthemum, owned by Mr R. Schnei
and handled by Peter Green, taking Best of Breed under judge Vinc
Perry at Green Mountain Dog Club, July, 1971

American Ch. Prospectblue Elizabeth takes Best of Breed at Sir Francis
Drake Kennel Club Show, California, September, 1972, when the author
was judge. Prospectblue Elizabeth was owned by Dr and Mrs Hugh
Jordan and Dick and Lorry Boerner

American Ch. Taralane's Beauregard Bleu making an excellent pillow for her young friend

Mr and Mrs R. Anderson's Nordic Champion Rollingsea Witchcraft, born 9th February, 1971, and photographed at 15 months. This young bitch has begun an outstanding show career, gaining her title of Nordic Champion at 10 months.

(*Left*) Mrs Grimwade using a simple spindle whilst Wrightway St. Andrew watches his wool being spun. (*Right*) Ch. Prospectblue Cindy pictured with her family, all of whom are wearing garments made from Cindy's combings

Mr and Mrs A. V. Sharpe's dog Dash, on one of his advertising assignments, seems quite at home with this little girl sitting firmly on his back

8

BREEDING

In general the public looks upon dog breeders as a race of rather odd people who are eccentric enough to keep a number of dogs solely for the purpose of breeding and selling them on a lucrative market. Alternatively, they consider breeders as persons with no other interest, who rarely look clean or tidy. This, of course, is nonsense, breeders cover a wide range of individual types and come from every walk of life, with the only thing in common being an interest in breeding dogs. There are those with a pet dog who decide it would be fun to have a litter of puppies; in fact many owners feel the urge to see their pet with puppies and think it will do her good. It is doubtful whether breeding one litter from a bitch will make any difference, because it will do neither good nor harm, but just be an interesting experience. It is often thought that an hysterical bitch will settle down if she has a litter, or that a bitch which habitually gets a phantom pregnancy will be cured, or that it will never get pyometra (an infected womb). If the breeding is not repeated several times throughout the life of the bitch, it will do little to guard against the possibility of pyometra. Certainly an hysterical bitch will just produce a percentage of hysterical puppies and, though she may slow down during the process, she will return to her normal temperament afterwards. As to phantom pregnancies, these are when a bitch imagines she has puppies and behaves as if in whelp. Often she has milk and is off colour when the puppies would be due, even though she has not been mated to a dog.

It is upsetting for her, and owners quite rightly feel sorry for a bitch behaving in this way. However, giving her the chance to have a litter will be unlikely to stop her having a phantom pregnancy next time. I knew of a Dandie Dinmont who never had a phantom until after she had produced a litter of puppies.

If a pet owner wants the joy of seeing her bitch with puppies and is willing to cope with the extra work involved, it is worth doing, providing there are enough good homes waiting for the resulting puppies. Old English Sheepdog puppies are utterly adorable and ready to captivate the hardest heart, but when selling them one must be sure the new owners really want a large and hairy dog.

Many people begin as pet owners breeding one litter, and then, becoming more interested and involved, they end up by acquiring more dogs. Eventually they find they have a small kennels and an absorbing hobby. These pet owners who get interested in breeding form one type of breeder.

Another type is the person who buys two or three bitches and has the intention of breeding from the beginning. It may be that they always wanted to do this and they have a strong love of the bobtail and in this case they will probably make good breeders striving to breed from good stock, arranging properly erected kennels and giving careful thought to the well being of the dogs, their feeding and exercising, etc. Happily, there are numerous breeders who strive to breed from the best stock and who give loving care; the bobtail is a sensitive creature and needs affection and reassurance as much as it needs food and a cosy bed. We look to these breeders to improve the breed and to keep to true type.

It is unfortunate that the label 'breeder' extends to include anyone who produces a litter of puppies, no matter how bad the conditions or how poorly they are reared. The fact that this is so, is very confusing to the public generally.

To the reader who is a newcomer to the breed, I cannot stress strongly enough the importance of finding the very best of homes for puppies. It is not enough to try to breed good stock and take pride in well reared puppies if insufficient thought is given to the homes where those puppies will go, whether for showing and breeding or for pets. It is worth meeting the people if possible, or if you are not certain about them, to make local enquiries.

Only keep as many dogs as you can look after comfortably, and it is better to breed less puppies than you can sell to good homes, rather than more.

For the pet owner with one bitch to mate, it is not a good idea to find the nearest pedigree Old English Sheepdog and to hope for the best, the attitude being that she is only a pet and it really does not matter too much. For any litter at all, the owner owes it to the breed to try and breed good puppies. A percentage of puppies from practically every litter born will later be used for breeding purposes and if the quality is not considered, this poor quality is there to be passed on to the next generation. Choose one of the well known and well tried stud dogs, or if there is progeny from one of these in your district, ascertain that it is a presentable dog, sound and with a good temperament, with no hereditary defects to pass on. If there is nothing of quality living near you, it is well worth going a journey for such an important mission as to find a good stud. There will be the choice of one of the Champions, or there are other good dogs who have not gained their title of Champion but have sired litters with excellent puppies. These you can only discover by following the dog shows and noting in the catalogue the breeding of lovely youngsters in the show ring. Some outstanding youngsters themselves may produce excellent puppies, but you would not be able to have proof of that until the litter is born. It would only be advisable to risk mating to a very young promising dog of 12–18 months if there was a history of outstanding breeding in the family of the dog as a whole, or if you know of a litter that was a success from such a dog.

If you are intending to establish a modest kennels, the foundation stock must be carefully chosen and I would advise beginning with one or two good bitches, rather than with a dog and a bitch as a pair from which to breed. A bitch is not mature and ready to breed until about two years old and every second or third season after that is how often she will be ready to breed again, as the bobtail is a large dog and takes time to mature, also the litters average about seven to eight puppies as a rule and it takes time for her to recover her resources. If you begin with a dog and a bitch, the dog will have to be kept away from her at the times you are not breeding and this is always quite a problem even if you have adequate space. Two bitches give you a chance to rest one whilst the other is having a litter and you can take them to a good stud dog when necessary. If you wish to have more bitches later on when you have had the experience of coping with two, then it may be wise to have a stud dog of your own or suitable bloodline.

It is useful to have your own dog and he will be able to be shown regularly whereas a bitch is out of the show ring when she is in season or when she is having puppies and in the latter case she will take months to get back in condition and to grow a full coat again. Even so, it takes careful arrange-ment of the kennelling and management to have a good stud dog and bitches, in order to have the dog relaxed and ready to show, because if he gets wind of a bitch in season he will most likely go off his food and pine to be with her, and with three or four bitches these times come around rather frequently. This is maddening at show times, if the dog looses weight and behaves badly, as his heart will not be in showing and you may as well stay at home as try to win with him in that frame of mind.

There is no simple recipe for how to breed the ideal dog. If this were the case, it would be easy, but it is possible to plan a breeding programme that should turn out good stock and this calls for careful planning, coupled with a bit of luck. Trying to breed an outstanding Champion is an everlasting challenge which entails much hard work and set backs and sometimes downright bad luck, but it is an absorbing task which will be packed with interest and rewarded with a thrilling triumph if you should succeed.

Assuming you have acquired one or two really good bitches, you will have something to show when they are ready and until you breed from them, and you will have worthy specimens to use for breeding. When choosing a stud dog, it is best to rely on a Champion or good dog from a good family; that is, a high standard of quality in brothers and sisters as well as good parents and grandparents, if possible. Sometimes an outstanding dog can be one star from a mediocre litter, from a family that did not make a habit of producing stars. It is better if there is a choice, to find a good one from a litter which is good all round and with a good background as this is more likely to produce puppies true to the high standard of the family generally. The occasional star from a mediocre background is not nearly so likely to sire a uniformally good litter.

Choose, if you can, a dog from a quality family and of a similar type to the bitch; preferably excelling in any point that she lacks. For instance, if the bitch lacks skull, then choose a dog of a similar type but with a good skull. When both dog and bitch have the same weakness, it will be accentuated in the offspring.

Years ago, when I first began looking for a stud dog for my bitch, there were so few to be found that there was very little choice and, having decided which would be the best, it was not too easy getting them mated partly because there was not enough regular work for the dogs and they were therefore inexperienced and, for the same reason, so were the owners. It was all very frustrating and real planning was impossible. Nowadays, with the tremendous increase in the breed, many of the dogs are used regularly and come from parents who were experienced so that their instinct and performance is totally different from those dogs of years ago. Breeders also are far more experienced and judge more cleverly when a bitch is ready.

The subject of breeding and genetics is a vast one and covers line-breeding and inbreeding and the introduction of an outcross, but I would advise any beginner to begin with well-chosen bitches as foundation stock and aim to mate them with Champions or good sound dogs of similar type. The close family breeding is very useful in establishing virtues and type, but should only be considered by the experienced breeder who realises all the risks as well as the benefits to be derived.

If you are aiming at quality, you must plan to rear your stock on the best of food and keep them in the very best conditions, and you should go to shows, particularly Championship shows, to assess your stock and find out if they really can hold their own in competition and to let the public and other breeders see what you have in your kennel. Never imagine that, as each puppy is fairly expensive, you will make a great deal of money because this is not so at all. Good housing and feeding will be expensive and travelling to shows will be very expensive both in time and money and if you plan to try to make your puppy a Champion, you will have a tremendous amount of travelling to do. It is a challenge and fun, but is very hard work and you will be lucky if, after a litter or two, you manage to pay most of your expenses.

After years of campaigning a dog or bitch and breeding from them, very few breeders find it in their heart to put these old faithfuls to sleep prematurely. A bitch should not be bred from after about seven years as an average and this means a long while when she will be a pensioner – a very welcome one and much loved no doubt, but an item on the debit side.

THE BROOD BITCH

When looking after a dog or bitch of any age I would advise keeping it in good hard condition; slim, but not too thin and certainly never overweight and this applies especially in the case of a brood bitch. A very fat bitch is not easy to get mated and, even if you are successful, it is unlikely that she will conceive. Ideally, a bitch should be in the peak of condition when she is to be mated and although she should not be bred before she is about two years old, it is best not to leave it more than a year after that before having a first litter. If it is left too long there may be some difficulty in getting her co-operation at mating time and obviously it is better for her to have a litter whilst her bone structure is able to give a little. Luckily bobtails on the whole rarely have whelping troubles and they normally make excellent mothers.

An Old English Sheepdog bitch usually comes in season for the first time when she is about 10 or 11 months old and thereafter at intervals of about six months and you will find that when she is coming in season dogs show special interest in sniffing her. The season will last about 21 days in all and at first she will have a clear discharge for two or three days and the vulva will swell up and bleeding begins. Once this coloured discharge begins, it will last about 12 days before paling in colour or even stopping completely for a while. It is noticeable that when the colour pales or stops temporarily, the vulva, which has become enlarged and hard, will soften and go slack. This is when your bitch is ready for mating if you wish her to have a litter, and you may expect her to be like this as early as the tenth day or as late as the eighteenth or nineteenth, but a very good average is the twelfth day. I have found that as the bitch grows older she is often ready later in the season, even if it was the twelfth day when she was younger.

If you wish to mate your bitch and have decided on a suitable stud dog, you should find out in advance from the owner whether it is convenient for you to use the dog and say when you anticipate your bitch beginning her season. Having made arrangements with the owner of the stud dog all you have to do is to let them know as soon as your bitch is showing colour, to warn them you will most likely want to come to have her mated in about twelve days. Obviously you must watch your bitch and be ready for the signs described above, bearing in mind it could be from the tenth day onward and, when you think the time is right, telephone to the stud owner to arrange to take your bitch at once.

Bitches are only fit for mating for a few days as a rule and in some cases for a very brief time, possibly in extreme cases only a few hours, but others will stand any day during the course of five or six days. It is, therefore, important to try and time it very correctly. If you take the bitch too early, the ova will not have descended into the Fallopian tubes ready for fertilisation, but if you go a day or two late there is a possibility that there will still be some ova to fertilise. It is to be hoped you time it neither early nor late, but just right and this way get the maximum litter from the mating.

If you have to travel a distance to the stud dog, rest your bitch for a while on arrival. Never let your bitch out of the car until you have contacted the owner of the stud dog and enquired where they would like you to take her. It is annoying to have a visiting bitch running freely where your dogs will be distracted with the scent, also there may be other dogs about who discover your bitch before she gets mated to the correct stud.

It is worth mentioning here that no form of deterrent should be used on the bitch prior to bringing her to be mated. There are various products such as 'Anti mate' to keep dogs away from a bitch in season, or amplex to take away the scent. It is the scent from the bitch that gives the right message to the dog so that it is a great mistake to use anything to rob her of this.

After your bitch has had a short rest on arrival, enquire from the owner of the stud dog where she can go to relieve herself before being introduced to the dog.

THE STUD DOG

As with the brood bitch, it is wise to have a stud dog in top condition, well fed, well muscled and never overweight. Do not feed the stud dog for some hours before he is used at stud as he will only be sick, but it is quite a good plan to give him an egg beaten up in a little milk, with a tablespoonful of glucose added, and he can have this about two hours before the bitch arrives.

It is usual to have some place set aside for stud work, such as a barn, garage or outhouse, where there is a clear space with no obstacles to bump into or fall on the dogs to put them off. It is up to the owner of the stud dog to be in command of the arrangements and, other than the owner of the bitch, it is best to have no one else around. The dogs want no distractions and the less talking the better, other than a gentle word of reassurance and that only if it is not done at a distracting moment. However badly the bitch behaves, do not scold her, just be patient and calm and ready to be helpful.

The bitch should be taken to the allotted place, on a collar and lead, and then the dog can be brought in and introduced to her. If the bitch does not take fright and really fly at him, her lead can be unloosed and they can have an opportunity to flirt for a short while, and this they do charmingly. If the bitch is ready she should stand and await the dog's advances. The majority of stud dogs have had experience of bitches who will flirt, but when he gets serious they panic and snap, so that it is prudent and helpful to hold the bitch's collar and be ready to hold her steady . . . A number of dogs and bitches mate naturally and easily but many bitches get overcome with the whole situation and keep sitting down and are anything but helpful, so that they may need someone to put a hand under them to keep them standing.

The dog will probably ride her several times before mating her and when this happens, once the dog's penis erects inside the vagina of the bitch, there is a band of muscles in the bitch which contract and hold him 'tied' there for anything from a few minutes to an hour or more, but fifteen to twenty minutes is an average. The dog, once tied, will usually pass one of his hind legs over the back of the bitch and turn to stand facing the opposite direction, so that they are back to back. During this time there must be supervision to ensure the bitch does not try to sit down and so injure the dog. Both parties are often very bored with this part of the proceedings.

Once the dog is released from the bitch, he should be returned quietly to his kennel to rest and the bitch can benefit from a pat to make her muscles contract and it is best to put her somewhere quietly. If you have come by car then she will probably be most at home lying there. Do not let her relieve herself for several hours.

After the services of the stud dog, while your bitch is resting, you should pay the stud fee, which is due at time of service, and in return you should receive a copy of the dog's pedigree. If, at the end of nine weeks, there are no puppies there is no legal obligation, but most stud owners allow the bitch a free service when next she is in season, if the dog is available and it is convenient.

The bitch should continue to be kept away from other dogs once she has been mated until her season has ended and therefore she will be kept fairly quietly for about a week. After that time, continue normal routine and there is no need to increase the diet until about five weeks later when you should have some idea as to whether she is in whelp. If she is hungry and you think she is expecting puppies, increase her diet gradually. For a bitch who normally eats 1 lb. 4 oz. or 1 lb. 6 oz. protein, plus biscuit meal and vitamins, by the time the litter is due, the diet will be 2 lb. to 2½ lb. with extra vitamins and extra calcium; be guided by her appetite and give more if she wants it, but not too much extra carbohydrates.

At six weeks there should be signs of the nipples swelling and a definite enlarging of the abdomen. It is between six and nine weeks that the greatest increase in size is noticeable and during that time she is unlikely to want to race about or jump, but avoid moments of great excitement which might make her leap about. As the bitch gets very heavy, several short walks are better than one or two longer walks and if you divide the food into three meals rather than one or two it will be more comfortable for her.

For the three weeks before the arrival of puppies the bitch should be living in the kennel where she will be whelping her puppies. If she already lives in a kennel that will adapt to house her and her puppies, as described in the chapter on housing, then it is simple. The period of gestation is 63 days, but it may be up to five days before this date or even two or three days after, so be prepared and watch for signs of her getting very near time, so that you will be on hand to see to her and to prepare the whelping bed. Most bitches go off their food a few days before whelping.

The normal sleeping platform must be scrubbed clean and a little disinfectant added to the water and this should be done on a good drying day about a few days before the puppies are due. When the bitch begins to get restless and pants a great deal, labour will be fairly soon, perhaps two or three hours or anything up to about 36 hours and during this time you can replace any normal bedding with a clean piece of sheeting, firmly tacked to the platform, or clean washed sacking will serve if you have no suitable old sheets. This forms a firm surface if she wants to scrape and pull on it when she has labour pains. Clean newspapers are useful spread on top of the sheeting as they are warm, absorbent and easily disposable.

If your bitch is a little restless and panting, but not very enthusiastically, it is possible to tell whether labour is imminent by taking the temperature. If the bitch is about to whelp her puppies, her temperature, which is normally 101.5°F. will fall to as low as 98°F. This will begin usually with the bitch shivering and straining and before long a puppy is born; first the water bag, with the puppy, and then the afterbirth. The bitch will normally see to everything herself, cleaning up and biting the cord and appearing to handle the newly born rather roughly, but in reality this helps to get the whelp breathing. Once you can hear the first cry of the newly born puppy, you know all is well and the important thing is to keep the kennel warm for the new arrival.

A dull emitter infra red lamp hung as low as possible, without being in reach of the bitch, is invaluable at any time of the year, even if for a summer litter you may not need it on for more than a few hours at a time. Newly born puppies must be kept warm and I keep a small box with a stone hot water jar, over which is a piece of warmed blanket, and when the bitch whelps other puppies those already born can be kept warm in this box.

Bitches vary quite a bit in their method of producing their puppies, some getting on with it and having the puppies at more or less regular intervals of twenty minutes or half an hour, others are equally satisfactory whelpers but seem to take much longer between the puppies and with a large litter it tends to drag on for hours. I had one bitch who was just like clockwork, she would be lying down panting and obviously about to whelp and then she would stand up, shiver, strain – only once – and produce a puppy. Having cleaned it up and settled down to nurse the new puppy, in quarter of an hour or twenty minutes, perhaps less, she stood again and went through the same routine, and this continued until she had the whole litter. Sometimes she would rest for up to an hour in the middle of the process but it was very businesslike and always followed the same pattern, until her last litter which came a little slower. Some bitches whelp in this manner

of standing up as they have the puppies but many lie down
to have them, and one bitch I still have prefers to have her
litter in a straw bed. She wriggles about to make a flat part
to lie in and pushes the rest of the straw in a high wall
around her, making it rather like an enormous nest and then
she lies down and never moves her position until her litter
is born and she is happily nursing them. This bitch would be
very unhappy if I tried to put the puppies on a hot water
bottle whilst she whelped the next one; she needs no assistance but I creep in to see how she fares and give her an
occasional drink of warm milk and glucose as I do to all my
bitches when there is a pause in the proceedings.

Difficulties with whelping are not usually associated with
the Old English Sheepdog, but one should be aware of the
possible exceptions in order to be prepared. When the bitch
begins in labour, she may strain weakly at first and then get
to work with more effort and produce a puppy. If she is
straining hard and it goes on for two hours with nothing happening, you should call your Veterinary Surgeon to see what
is wrong.

Sometimes a bitch will begin quite well and whelp several
puppies and then rest and make no more effort and this may
just be a longish rest between, but if she continues with no
contractions, this is known as uterine inertia and for this you
should call your Veterinary Surgeon as he can give an injection which should begin the contractions again. If the injection does not have the desired result the bitch will probably have to have a Caesarian operation. Uterine inertia can
occur in any bitch but is more common with the older bitch.

Occasionally, instead of the puppy arriving as it should
with the head appearing first, it is presented with hind legs
·first and this is known as a breech birth and, although many
puppies are born arriving this way without too much difficulty, sometimes help is necessary. Often when a bitch is
straining to have a breech puppy, the membrane opens and
the legs are·protruding and in this case it is possible with the

aid of a piece of clean towel to grip the legs firmly and draw them forward and downward. Once the bag is broken the puppy should be rescued immediately in case it gets drowned.

Sometimes when the new puppy is born the bitch will open the bag and bite the cord, but the puppy lies as if dead and she is not interested in licking it or bothering with it. If you offer it to her she may lick it and get it breathing but if not you can use a clean rough towel and firmly rub the puppy in a circular motion against the growth of the coat. If the friction does not get it breathing, there may be excessive mucus in the puppy's breathing tract. In this case, rotate the puppy several times slowly backwards as if on an axis at a point on the body behind the forelegs; mucus will most likely drain out and if you then hold it head downwards and give a gentle shake this will help clear the mucus. If the puppy is still not breathing, open it's mouth and pull the tongue forward and put your mouth over the puppy's nose and mouth and blow gently. Then give a little pressure either side of the ribs to expel the air and repeat the performance about four times per minute. The idea being to rotate the puppy and get away as much mucus as possible and then give artificial respiration to get the puppy breathing. Once it gives a little cry and is living the puppy will transform, turning a good pink colour and losing the blue look it had previously. If you do not wish to put your mouth over the puppy's nose and mouth, you can use a piece of cardboard or rubber tubing and using one end to encase the puppy's nose and mouth you blow through the other end.

Do not imagine that it is not worth bothering to save a limp and apparently dead puppy, you will be more than repaid when you hear that first cry and see the puppy come to life. I have saved a number of puppies in my time and always I experience the thrill of excitement when it utters that first cry and I know it is alive at last and can join the rest of the litter.

It is advisable to notice whether the bitch passes an after-

birth after each puppy because at the end it helps to know
that she has expelled the last afterbirth and that there is
nothing left behind to cause trouble. This is difficult to
notice very often as the bitch eats each membrane or bag
in which the puppy arrives and she also eats the afterbirths.
This sounds rather peculiar but it is the natural thing for a
bitch to do and in fact it would be almost impossible to stop
her.

Providing the bitch is no longer straining and seems quite
content with her family she has probably finished whelping.
If by any chance there is an afterbirth left behind then you
will soon find that she will be restless and spring a temperature and you should call your Veterinary Surgeon; luckily
this rarely happens.

A fact one must realise as being a possibility, but which is
luckily a very rare occurrence, is that the bitch, under certain
circumstances, could die leaving puppies to survive her. In
this case, or if the bitch should live but have no milk, the
puppies would have to be kept warm and fed on one of the
milk products on the market being as near as possible a sub-
stitute for bitch's milk and the feeding would have to be a
little and often. It was always considered necessary to feed
orphan puppies every two hours with feeds at night time as
well as the day, but more recently I have heard of puppies being fed every three or four hours and in addition a vitamin
preparation being given by means of a feeding tube straight
into the stomach and this would undoubtedly make the task
of bringing up orphan puppies very much easier.

When a bitch is looking after her new born puppies she
will lick them around the genital area in order that they will
urinate and expel any waste, which she will immediately
clean up and this happens for about two weeks when they
no longer need assistance in this way. When rearing puppies
without the help of the dam it is necessary to simulate this
action by gently sponging the area with damp warm cotton
wool, or a small piece of sponge damped in warm water.

Having considered the various troubles that can occur, I may say that a normal healthy bitch, bred from in good form, rarely poses any of these problems. It may well be that you will come down one morning a few days before the litter is due and find that during the night or early morning, your bitch has whelped a fine sturdy litter and they all look astonishingly well and content. This does happen and many bitches prefer to whelp on their own, though I like to look in from time to time – discreetly not to disturb her – just to be sure all is going well. Other bitches appear to derive comfort from someone they know very well being on hand. It is therefore best to study your bitch and do what she likes, providing there are no problems.

9

CARE OF THE NEW PUPPIES

Once the litter is born, providing you are satisfied that all the puppies are suckling properly, you can have a quiet day or two before the tails have to be docked. This should be done on the third or fourth day unless there are weakly puppies and a little delay is advisable, and it is important that your Veterinary Surgeon knows that the entire tail is to be removed, leaving no stump. At the same time as the docking is done, it is necessary to remove all dew claws as these can be troublesome later on when they grow long and get caught in the long leg featherings. Some puppies have no hind dew claws others have no dew claws on the forelegs, whilst occasionally a puppy will have unsightly double dew claws on the hind legs.

Many breeders spend a great amount of time weighing puppies when they are born and regularly each week and at one time I did so but found there is little to be gained by this, though I would keep an eye on the weight of a very backward small puppy when trying to build it up to get it nearer to the size of the rest of the litter by adjusting the feeding. There are sometimes one or two puppies which are weaker than the rest of the litter and if left to nature the big ones grow bigger and the little ones get practically no milk at all, and grow weaker and if they grow too weak they are slow to move and are liable to get stepped on by the dam. To help these weak puppies in their first few days you can easily put them on to a teat and protect them from the strong puppies who make a habit of coming up from below, rather like busy little submarines on a mission intent on pushing the weak puppy off and suckling in its place. With a large litter, if there are not enough teats for all the puppies, it is a great help to the bitch if one or two of the stronger puppies take it in turns to feed on a bottle about four times a day; I use a baby's premature feeding bottle for this purpose. Supplementary feeding is easier once the puppies can lap which should be at two to two and a half weeks.

After the day when dew claws are removed and tails are docked, it is quite peaceful for about two weeks as the bitch should see to her family and you will have to see that she builds up her intake of food and drink, but do this gradually or she may scour and this would mean a set back. I give the bitch food or a drink of milk, or milk and glucose, every two hours and, with a litter of six to eight puppies, by the time the puppies are three weeks old when they are making a big demand on their dam, she will be eating about 4 lb. meat, two eggs, biscuit meal, vitamins with extra calcium and three pints of milk. If the bitch has plenty of milk and not more than five or six puppies, I leave it until they are three and a half weeks old to feed anything to the whelps, but if it is a litter of more than six puppies, they get milk or a little beef at two and a half weeks of age. The beef must be tender and prepared by scraping with a tablespoon and begin by giving half a teaspoonful for a feed; the amount can be increased every few days.

By the time the puppies are four weeks old they should be able to eat four meals per day – two cereal and milk feeds and two meat feeds – and they will suckle at least twice per day as well. By this time they will be running about and be at a fascinatingly interesting age.

As it is wise to feed each puppy in a separate dish with the correct amount of food, I have made a feeder for this purpose with a partition for each dish, and at about four weeks old the puppies are ready to stand at their dishes in the feeder.

If there is one slow eater you can watch and protect him from the others until the dish is empty.

The feeder is quite easy to make and is well worth the trouble as it is almost impossible to organise a number of puppies at different dishes especially if you have no one about to help you. The feeder I made consists of eight compartments each housing one puppy and its dish. The puppy stands on the ground with a partition separating it from his neighbours and the dish is on a little platform.

You will need a piece of wood 15 in. wide and 32 in. long to form the platform. Cut a narrow groove down the centre of the platform lengthways. Have ready three pieces of wood each measuring 10 in. by 29 in. to form upright sections across the platform, and another piece of light wood or hardboard 32 in. by 15 in. to make the centre division as in Fig 8A.

Cut three slots in the centre division, each wide enough to accommodate the thickness of the wood in the cross sections (i.e. the 10 in. by 29 in. pieces) and make these slots to measure 7 in. as in Fig. 8B.

Now take the three pieces of wood required for the cross-sections and cut a slot in each of these to accommodate the width of the centre division and measuring 3 in. See Fig. 8C.

Next fit the centre division (with slots facing downwards) to the cross-sections matching the slots. The centre division fits in the groove of the platform and stands upright as do the cross-sections. These can be fixed firmly by screwing or nailing from the underside of the platform, and it is advisable to glue the centre division in place in its groove.

A coat of paint gives a finished look to the feeder and makes it easier to keep clean. Bakelite flower pot saucers make ideal first size dishes and to keep them in place a small beading around the edge of the feeder is a help.

There is no doubt that it is an advantage to have a litter born in the spring as they come out in warmish weather for their early outings and should get plenty of sunshine, fresh

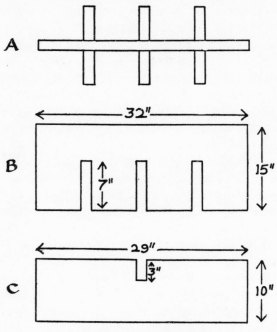

FIG. 8 Making a puppy feeder

air and freedom during the months ahead. When first hardening off a young litter, you can let them run about after their feed and as soon as they begin lying about and getting sleepy it is wise to put them back in the kennel to have a sleep. Between four and six weeks the puppies will grow up tremendously and at six weeks if the weather is warm they can have the door open into a sheltered run so that they can go in and out as they please. I never leave them to lie about in rain or an east wind at any age, but other than that they have a great amount of freedom.

During the period three and a half to five weeks they will have become independent of their dam, apart from perhaps suckling once or even twice a day, but between five and six weeks she should finish with them altogether as however much she appears to want to see the puppies, it will pull her down in health if she goes on trying to suckle these strong demanding puppies. It is wise to feel the bitch's milk supply and if one or two quarters are filling uncomfortably with milk, then put one strong puppy with her to milk it off just to make the bitch comfortable. As soon as the puppies cease to suckle the supply of milk should dwindle and you can help this by giving the bitch less milk drinks and gradually scaling down the meat diet for a while as well. I find most nursing bitches suddenly appear thin when the puppies are about six or seven weeks old and to counteract this continue with extra food – carbohydrates, eggs and dried fish and some meat, which helps build up her condition again without being a milk making diet. Once the milk has disappeared she can go back on her normal diet but with one and a half times the usual amount until her condition is right to scale it down.

I believe in cutting puppies' nails every week until they run about on rough ground to wear them down themselves. Long nails are very painful to a bitch when the puppies suckle, also by cutting the nails from an early age you are preparing for the neat feet of the future. Cut straight across the tip of the nail but avoid cutting too near the quick as this would be painful to the puppy. Test each nail carefully with your finger and snip off any sharp part that would scratch the dam.

Before puppies go to their new homes they should be wormed twice, with two weeks between the doses, and according to what worming medicine is given they can be wormed just before six weeks and again two weeks later, or with some preparations they can be wormed at four weeks and six weeks, which is what I advise as the sooner they are cleared of any worms the sooner they will get maximum benefit from the food and care you give.

It is a busy time when the puppies are independent of their dam and they are wanting five or six meals a day and at this stage their house needs clean bedding very frequently. If the weather is good and they can run out they will not soil the bedding very much in the day time, but at night with seven or eight puppies they get very busy in this direction and it is important to keep the kennel as sweet and clean as possible. The young puppies smell so wonderful if housed in clean wheat straw with wood shavings and sawdust underneath to absorb the moisture.

A useful piece of equipment for when the puppies are running about outside their kennel is a portable run which folds away when not in use and can be attached to the kennel temporarily. In our case the whelping kennel is next to a wall so that the wall forms one side of the run and all that is necessary is one long section (10 ft.) and one short section (5 ft.) of garden fencing about 3 ft. high. These two sections are hinged together and on the front of the kennel there is a strip of wood to form a slot next to the doorpost. The kennel is situated on concrete and the long piece of fencing can fix in the slot at one end. At the other end of the longer piece is the hinge and thus the second piece of fencing is used as a gate which shuts and fixes with a clasp fitted on the wall. A concrete block outside the long fencing at the hinged corner helps to keep it steady. If the kennel was not by a wall, the same idea could be employed by means of a second section 10 ft. long fitted to the other side of the front of the kennel. This hinged fencing is used in various ways to keep the puppies penned in various parts of the run as they grow and need more room.

After the early care and the weaning the puppies will soon be ready to be sent to their new homes. There are many excellent homes and as many really bad ones and it is vital to make sure that your puppies all go to really good homes. I have heard of puppies being sent to their new homes as young as five weeks old but this is far too young. The puppy can benefit from staying in the nest until about seven weeks and in very cold weather or if it has to go a long journey

eight weeks is a better age, but if it is left much after eight
weeks the puppy will be too attached to its surroundings and
will find it more difficult to adjust.

It is usual for the breeder to register the litter and to sell
the puppies with their registration certificates and transfer
forms and for the benefit of the puppy as well as the new
owner information should be given to them about the diet
and any other help they appear to need. So many people
having a puppy for the first time, or not having had one for
some years, have little idea about feeding and housing their
new pet and they will appreciate your help.

If any of the puppies is to be exported, it is necessary to
arrange this through a reliable Shipping Agent unless you
live near Heathrow and can make your own arrangements.
For most breeders a reliable Agent is important and if the
export is for Europe the puppy should be at least nine weeks,
for Canada and America where the journey is longer and
may lead to delays twelve weeks is a better age. A puppy
destined for Australia should be even older as it is a long sea
voyage because no dogs are allowed into Australia or New
Zealand by air and on arrival they have a period of quaran-
tine.

A Veterinary Certificate of Health has to accompany a
puppy being exported and the new owners will want you to
furnish them with an Export Pedigree for which an application form for Export Pedigree has to be completed and sent
to the Kennel Club. That is all that is necessary for Canada
or America though on arrival they will have to be vaccinated
against rabies and in Canada they have to be tatooed with
identity. Some countries including Scandinavia and Australia
require a leptospirosis test before an animal can be admitted,
and this can be done by your Veterinary Surgeon and sent to
the Ministry of Agriculture, Fisheries & Food at Surbiton,
Surrey, for testing.

One puppy being exported to Port Cartier, Saguenay
County, Canada gave me a very nerve-wracking time. A

flight had to be booked to Montreal where the puppy would be changed to another plane to finish the journey to Port Cartier. The people buying the puppy wrote to say they were delighted to know I had one to send to them as their friends had already acquired a puppy from me and they had fallen in love with the breed. They added that they would very much appreciate it if I would keep the puppy for another six weeks as they were going to Bermuda on holiday and wanted the puppy immediately on their return. This seemed simple enough and I agreed but warned them the air fare would be more as the puppy would be that much bigger. Three weeks before the date of sending, the Shipping Company telephoned to say that the cost would leap up to £85 if the puppy did not fit in a certain sized travelling kennel. I measured the puppy and wondered would he fit in the smaller kennel when the time came? Another week passed; he would be a tight fit, they grow so fast at this age. Another week and I knew it would have to be the larger kennel; at least I did warn them he would cost more. But this was not the only problem as the Shipping Company then discovered that the flight from Montreal to Port Cartier could not accommodate the larger kennel and they could only book the flight to Montreal. It was no good running the tape measure over him again as he was a big chap and still growing and he must have that large kennel. It was a worrying moment and I felt I would never make a rash promise to keep a fast growing puppy again. Eventually I telephoned the people as soon as they arrived home from their holiday and had all my facts ready as £3 per three minutes made me nervous of not saying it quickly enough, but I need not have worried as they were charmed to speak to me and as it happened their Company had an aircraft on a flight between Montreal and Port Cartier and they could arrange to meet the puppy at Montreal and let him travel as a V.I.P. right to his destination. Lucky puppy and he had a wonderful home waiting for him.

The family who bought this puppy visited England in

1970 and came down to Cornwall to look us up and meet the rest of the dogs. They brought many photographs of their dog and their friend's dog and they told an amusing story of their dog in the snow, which showed a tremendous sense of fun which so many bobtails have. The snow is thick and dry for many months throughout the winter and the dog loved to play in it. He went out one afternoon and his owner heard bumps and noises and thought her son and his pals were at home from school and playing about, but on looking out there was no sign of anyone, not even the dog. She went out to look for him and then there was a thud as the dog slid off the roof and landed bump in the snow. Delighted with his performance, he galloped up a snowdrift by the garage and climbed up the snow covered roof and along the house roof and slid down on to the roof of a dormer window, then had another slide down off the roof and bumped down in the snow again. Panting with excitement, he repeated the performance four times whilst his astonished owner watched.

Thereafter the dog made a habit of sliding off the roof and when the snow began to melt as long as the snowdrift was high enough he climbed up on to the roof of the dormer window and lay there surveying the scene. This was his favourite haunt until the snowdrift melted and he had to forget about roof climbing for that winter.

It warms my heart and certainly should touch the heart of any breeder to hear news of the stock they have sold. Apart from hearing of any winning in the show ring, it is so reassuring to know that a home has turned out to be a good one, giving the dog a happy, healthy life in conditions where it is appreciated.

When choosing homes for a litter of puppies, remember to look at it from the puppy's point of view. The new owner should be able to afford to buy the puppy in the first place and then keep it well fed and housed, but creature comforts alone do not make a happy home. The people should be

Some owners tend to
grow like their dogs....

genuine dog lovers who are willing to exercise in wet as well
as fine weather and who see the dog is properly cared for at
all times. A family with children can be ideal, or it can be
sheer cruelty for the dog as some children are allowed to pull
a puppy about and give it no peace. One should be satisfied
that the new owners have the sense and patience required to
teach their children to handle the puppy gently, with no teasing and to let it sleep peacefully and undisturbed when it
needs rest.

I have heard it said that if a person gives a high price for
a dog it is sure to be well cared for, but I do not agree. In
some cases the dog is left to servants to look after and it may
be they love him or they may almost dislike dogs and find a
large, hairy monster more than they can endure. Sometimes
the servants love the dog and it returns this affection which
it may not get so much from the owners and they resent this
situation so that the dog suffers.

I know of one family where the children evidently had more money than most and they bought their father a bobtail puppy as a Christmas present. When I asked whether the father wanted the puppy they said 'Oh no, but we thought it would be fun.' It is so important that everybody having a puppy not only wants it, but wants it very much indeed. If a couple wish to buy a puppy they must both want it, otherwise any lack of harmony arising from its presence later on will react on the dog.

A sad situation arose with a puppy bought through dealers by a family who lived well and could afford all the food and requirements, but the poor little fellow was very unhappy to the point of not thriving and appearing ill. It was very puzzling but I talked to some members of the family and discovered that there was great jealousy as to who should feed and exercise the puppy, though none of them really wanted to do this regularly, but only when they felt like it. The result was that with nothing approaching regular routine and no security it was sensitive enough to pine and no one realised anything was wrong; they thought he was backward and dull.

If a family is wanting a bobtail and the children appear happy and reasonably disciplined it is likely the dog will settle in happily with them, as caring for a puppy is rather similar to bringing up children. They need a comfortable bed, good nourishing food, security and love, with a certain amount of discipline.

It certainly behoves a breeder to tell people what is entailed in keeping a bobtail and if at the end of it they are still as keen to have one, all should be well.

When a puppy does go to its new home, it is a good plan to keep in touch with the new owners and encourage them to turn to you for advice so that if there are any problems you can help to make things easier for them and for the puppy.

10

TRAINING

HOUSE-TRAINING A PUPPY

Always put the puppy into the garden for house-training by using the same door, and it should be given an opportunity to be clean on awakening and after each meal. If the puppy goes out through the same door on each of these occasions it will soon learn to run to the door and ask to go out. A very young puppy cannot control its bladder and it will get excited when playing and will make a puddle about every fifteen minutes so that you have to be aware of this and forestall it.

The routine of the puppy in its new home will consist of eating, sleeping and playing, much like a human baby and if one remembers to put it out at the appropriate moments in a very short time it will be clean during the day. At night time it is more difficult as no very young puppy can be dry all night. If a thick wad of newspaper is left just inside the door through which it is used to going out to be clean, the puppy will run to the door and as this does not open, it will almost certainly make a puddle on the newspaper and this can be picked up very easily in the morning. By fifteen or sixteen weeks the Old English Sheepdog puppy should be dry and clean both night and day.

On bringing a young puppy into its new home, it will be sure to miss its brothers and sisters and although some puppies settle in a couple of nights with no more than an occasional howl of misery, others create a big disturbance, particularly if they have gone to a family who make a fuss of them during the day. At some time during each day the puppy should be left in its bed and alone as this is good training, not only for night time, but for the times when it will have to stay at home whilst the family goes out. If a puppy is not trained to stay quietly in its bed or kennel, then the time will come when a dog sitter will have to be installed on occasions when all humans are out at once; much like parents find a baby sitter.

When the puppy is left alone, if it cries and barks, take no notice for the first ten minutes and if the crying and barking continues then go to the door, do not open it, but use a very cross voice and tell the puppy to 'Be quiet at once.' If you enter the kennel or room to do this it becomes a social call and the puppy learns that a fine rumpus of a noise brings you running in, so stay outside the door and be very strict with your voice. If these admonishings do nothing to improve the situation, try another method. For this, time the silence between barking outbursts and when it is quiet for five minutes go in and say 'that was better' – be quite pleased but do not make too much praise at this stage; then busy yourself near the dog for a short while so that he gets the pleasure of your company but is not being made too much of just yet, and then come away again. Repeat the process and try to increase the time of the silence, you will have won the battle once the puppy has learned that when he is quiet you come back to him and this will make him happy, but when he is noisy you never come. I reckon to cure a noisy dog in two days with this method and have done it successfully a number of times.

When training a dog or puppy, try to do it all by tone of voice; a smack is practically never necessary, unless the dog has done something outrageous and then it must not be chastised with the hand, as the hand is a kind thing to fondle the dog and to handle it, not to make it cower away.

TEACHING A PUPPY TO COME

If you begin by associating the word 'come' with an encouraging happy voice, not a demanding 'come', but almost with excitement in your voice and do it at first when the puppy wants to come. For instance a good time to choose is when the dog's dinner is ready. Let the puppy (we will call him Ben) go out and whilst it is running about, you show the dinner dish and call an encouraging 'Ben, come', and with a dinner in the offing he will sure to come at once.

Further lessons can be when it is playtime and at first only call when you think there is a fair chance of the puppy obeying; always praise the right response. Repetition is the way to get any training remembered and only teach one command at a time, and repetition means a few times not overdoing the repeating to the point of boredom.

When teaching a puppy to 'come' never go towards the puppy, but if he does not appear to be coming turn and go away from him and call the command 'Ben come' again and most likely he will come after you. In a couple of weeks a puppy should get very good at coming when called, enjoying the praise he gets for doing it. Most bobtails learn to come very easily, but if there is any difficulty and the puppy is a bit wayward, it may be necessary to have him on a long leash, which can be tweaked to remind him to come, or he can even be hauled back on a leash, but once you give a command to come the puppy must obey.

WALKING ON A LOOSE LEAD

When the puppy is about ten to twelve weeks old and has had a slip lead on for a few times, the training can begin. A slip lead is lighter and more comfortable for a young puppy than a leather collar and lead, the weight of which worries most puppies and makes them scratch at the collar more often than not.

Hold the end of the lead in your right hand and pass it in

front of you to control half way down with the left hand, the puppy to walk at your left side. Every time the puppy gets ahead, call him and say 'Ben heel', turn to the right and at the same time tweak the lead with your left hand, this will put the puppy once more on your left and slightly behind you. After a while he will begin to realise he never does get ahead because of the way you turn to the right when you give the command 'Ben heel' and tweak the lead to gain his attention. As soon as there is an improvement and he keeps more or less beside you, the turns can be made only when he forges ahead and a tweak of the lead and command 'Ben heel' should check his creeping forward.

If a puppy is subsequently taught to walk at heel on the right of the handler it can be on the inside position when walking on country roads and facing the oncoming traffic.

TRAINING TO SIT AND STAY

To get a dog to sit, if it is to be a showman, is best not done by pressing down on his rear, or when the judge is examining him in the ring and testing the rear quarters, the dog will probably sit when he should stand. It is quite simple to get a puppy to sit by holding the collar under his chin with your left hand and gently pushing up and back. Meanwhile, the right hand (which might have a titbit and therefore the puppy thinks it is worth watching) is raised also up and back about a foot above the puppy's head; most puppies sit back on their haunches as they watch your right hand travelling up and back and after a few commands 'Ben sit' as you do this, it is no longer necessary to help with the left hand on the front of the collar. Occasionally a puppy just moves backward instead of sitting and in this case position him where there is a wall behind him and automatically he will sit. Once again remember to give plenty of praise when he does the right thing and disregard any false starts.

My training for 'sit' often occurs when I am waiting for

FIG. 9 Training a dog to 'sit'

the breakfast toast : I stand by and put my hand up and back
with the command 'Ben sit' and after two or three successful
times I reward the puppy with a piece of toast or a crust, and
it happens without appearing to be a lesson.

Once the 'sit' is thoroughly mastered 'stay' is not very difficult. With the puppy sitting, I hold either side of the collar
or slip lead and say 'Ben, stay' giving a final gentle but firm
pressure before I let go and step back two paces. Keep saying
'stay' and then return to the puppy. Praise him. If he moves
begin again. If he was very good I take three paces back
next time. Each time I give a lesson I begin with stepping
back two paces and then improve on the distance until he
is pretty sure to do the right thing. Once you can leave a
puppy ten yards away, you can do a recall 'Ben come' and
this helps the 'come' command again.

Living in the country we get our share of mud in wet weather and the 'sit and stay' is very useful at times when I want to feed animals in a muddy place or to shut a gate which is surrounded by mud and I do not want the dogs to follow. I call them in and tell them to sit and stay and they really look charming, sitting in a group, waiting patiently for my return. It will have kept them from being plastered in mud and at the same time will have made use of the little bit of obedience training they all get. For the benefit of getting them used to other animals I take at least one dog with me when feeding hens and other animals and they learn quickly to sit in the field awaiting my return as I do not take them in the run with me.

If a puppy is taught to come when called, to walk on a loose lead and then to sit and stay, it will be easy to control and be well behaved enough to be a pleasure. Once these first simple commands are mastered thoroughly, there is just one more command which is very useful on many occasions and that is 'wait'. This is different from 'stay' which follows 'sit' as it applies to the dog in motion and means he must stop or wait instantly. It is very useful when you wish to catch up with your dog to put him on a lead, or when he is free and a car is approaching. If he is tempted to give chase to something you can forestall it with 'wait'. To teach this, have the dog on a lead and walk him at heel and at regular intervals you stop suddenly and say 'Ben wait', at the same time jerking back on the lead. Go on a few paces and repeat the performance and in a short time he will get the idea. Later he will not require jerking with the lead and eventually he will stop when free and given the command at a distance. Too much obedience work can take away the sparkle of a dog, that extra lively look of joy and interest which is worth so much in the show ring, so that you must assess how your dog has reacted, whether it is an extra lively dog who can do with a bit more discipline, or whether it has become quiet enough. Probably most of the dogs who lose their sparkle are

H

given far too much obedience practice by owners who are over keen to get their dog perfect. Given normal practice the dog enjoys his obedience work very much and benefits from the lessons and the owner is reqarded with a well-behaved dog.

11

SPINNING BOBTAIL WOOL
AND PUBLICITY

The combings of various breeds of dogs can be saved and
spun for knitting wool or woven into material, but the
long hair of the Old English Sheepdog, with its woolly undercoat, makes it particularly suitable for this purpose. A number
of owners have saved the combings in the hope of getting
someone to spin them, or have tried their hand at using a
spinning wheel, an art which requires a great amount of
practice and patience to get a reasonably evenly spun
wool.

The North Western Old English Sheepdog Club brought
out a Year Book in 1955 in which the foreword was written
by the late Miss E. M. Flint, who was a dedicated breeder
and exhibitor for many years under the prefix 'Newcote'.
A photograph accompanying her article showed Miss Flint
wearing a skirt and full length coat woven from combings
from her dogs. The last paragraph of her foreword stated:
'The spinning and weaving of the Old English Sheepdog's
hair combings does not seem to have been thought of in the
early days. The first lot I had spun (to knit a jumper) I had
to send to a Crofter in Scotland to get done. About 1937 the
Somerset Weavers Institute made me up cloth from the combings. It made a beautiful cloth and I had a skirt and long
coat made from it. In the accompanying photograph I am
seen wearing it, whilst out walking with "Newcote Blossom-
kin". I still have this coat, it is in good repair, and I wore it
most of last winter.' Surely a tribute to the hard wearing
qualities that a coat could last for so many years.

Some time ago I was benched next to Mr and Mrs David Grimwade, when they were showing their dog Wrightway St Andrew and I was fascinated to watch Mrs Grimwade using a simple spindle to spin the dog's combings. This primitive and slow method of spinning proved an interesting hobby but became rather tedious and she decided to go to classes to learn how to use a spinning wheel, resulting in a speeding-up of the process, and the quantity of wool greatly increased. The next step is to weave this wool into material from which a skirt can be made but before embarking on weaving the skirt length Mrs Grimwade is practising by weaving a hearth rug, and this rather novel idea should prove a subject of interest and of amusement as the bobtail does get likened to a moving hearthrug on occasions! When the weaving of material is completed and the skirt made up, it will be unique in that Mrs Grimwade will have done it all by her own effort through every process from combing the dog to stitching the skirt.

There is a most intriguing story of Cindy, the only dog and family pet belonging to Mr Michael Garnett and it is certain he, his wife and their children have had more interest and fun out of Cindy than they imagined possible. In the first place they decided that a rampaging bobtail would not be much pleasure and Mr Garnett took her to Obedience training classes, where she reached a high standard and they were rewarded by having a well-behaved dog in the family. It was then decided to enter her in the show ring and they had the thrill and excitement of her gaining her title; she became Champion Prospectblue Cindy.

Most owners would have been satisfied having obedience trained their pet and made her a Champion in the show ring, but it did not work out like that for the Garnett family. Mr Garnett is a Director of a woollen and worsted manufacturing company in Bradford but he never considered spinning Cindy's hair until a friend in the trade, seeing him grooming, teased him about wasting the hair and challenged him to make a respectable looking piece of cloth from Old English Sheepdog's combings. It is surprising what a challenge will do and he set to work to save the combings, keeping the white separate from the grey. With spinning, weaving and finishing machinery at his disposal, he had the combings spun into wool – white wool and grey wool – and from 15 lb. of hair they produced 17 yards of fabric 30 in. wide.

By this time he thought what a tremendous joke it would be to his associates in the textile industry if a well tailored jacket was made from this material and this was done in February 1967. It was a very fine jacket indeed. When news of this remarkable jacket spread around, a large gathering of journalists and photographers came to the Mill to report on Cindy and the jacket and when Mr Garnett went on business to Australia and New Zealand a few days later, the story of the jacket had already reached them. He was interviewed on *Town and Around* radio programmes in Australia and New Zealand as well as on Jack de Manio's programme in England. They featured on Television in *Blue Peter*. Fan mail poured in from all over the world, with the majority of reactions being humorous. On one occasion Mrs Garnett answered the telephone and was questioned about Cindy and the jacket and to her astonishment at the end of the conversation the caller said he was speaking from Denver, Colorado and thanked her for talking on the air to the people of America!

Subsequently, from a larger amount of combings, material was made in block check which was dyed and made into a skirt for Mrs Garnett and tailored coats for their little girls, once again with remarkable results and it is difficult to imagine that any of the articles were made from Old English Sheepdog's combings. Made as an answer to that challenge, they created a tremendous amount of interest and publicity but, as may be imagined, they were not a commercial proposition and in spite of being offered combings from all kind of pets as well as 'Long, brown cow tails (disinfected) . . .' and reindeer hair, etc., the Mill continues with the normal traditional trade.

Publicity for the breed has come from films and television appearances of various bobtails, and the story of the jacket and Cindy must certainly have added its own particular brand of publicity.

The fact that the Old English Sheepdog has been adopted as the dog advertising Dulux paint has had an important impact on the breed. Whereas some years ago the majority of people would look at a bobtail and wonder what it was, the appearance over the past ten years of Mr and Mrs A. V. Sharpe's dog 'Dash' posing in advertisements in the press and on television, has done much to educate the public on the subject. Furthermore, this well-groomed and attractive character has charmed the public and helped to cause an ever-increasing demand for puppies, which will grow up to look like Dash.

In 1971 a competition was organised to find an assistant for Dash as he is creeping on in years and the six finalists were invited to stay in London for final tests, which included a five-minute screen test for each dog. The winners were announced at a champagne reception held at the Cafe Royal in Regent Street and Mr Norman Harrison's Lord Digby was the winner with my Rollingsea Viceroy runner-up. It was a great occasion and one to be remembered by all the finalists. Whilst the object was to choose an assistant for Dash, the press and photographers were present and, as well as the paint, our breed had its share of publicity once again.

Having had good publicity with the attendant increase in the demand for the breed, an even greater responsibility devolves on breeders to satisfy themselves that the would-be purchasers of their stock really do want a large heavily coated animal to demand their affection and attention for many years. It is a sad fact that publicity tends to increase the number of people who get fired with enthusiasm to have one of these dogs, without giving enough consideration to what it entails. No doubt they see a beautiful bobtail in the press or on television and they buy hastily but loose interest when the novelty wears off. Luckily with the interest resulting from publicity there is also a big increase in the number of genuine admirers of the breed ready to give an excellent home where the novelty does not wear off.

After a few years of increased popularity in the breed, it became apparent there was a growing number of unwanted and neglected bobtails to be found and there is now an organisation called The Bobtail Rescue Society, the aim of which is to take in any sadly treated bobtails and care for them before finding them suitable kind homes.

COMMON DISEASES AND AILMENTS

The average bobtail is not delicate or difficult to rear but luckily is normally a sturdy creature blessed with good health. Of the five main abnormalities inherited by dogs, there are certainly two which affect a percentage of our breed and these are Entropian and Hip Dysplasia.

Entropian is when the eyelids and eyelashes turn in towards the eye and cause great discomfort as the eyelashes irritate the surface of the eyeball, causing inflammation and a watering eye. If neglected, the sight can ultimately be affected. A simple operation will put the matter right but one should never breed from dogs suffering from this defect as it is considered hereditary.

Hip Dysplasia is what the name suggests – *dys* means bad and *plasia* means form; so it is a badly formed hip joint. If the socket is shallow and the head of the femur does not fit as snugly as it should, in time it shows signs of wear. If the case is very slight it would be impossible to detect without an X-ray. In severe cases the head of the femur gets misshapen, often getting progressively worse and ultimately arthritis sets in. With severe cases the condition is evident when the dog is moving and usually it is accompanied by a certain amount of pain. The dog will sit or lie down more than other dogs and there is a tendency to rest one hind leg, if it is only in the one joint, and to carry it very close to the other. If both joints are affected the legs are to be found very close together and very weak looking. The dog will sit with the weight taken by the front legs instead of resting comfortably back as it should. When the dog is standing, if one places a hand gently over each hip joint, it is possible to rock the hind quarters gently from left to right and back again, and if the joints are in an advanced stage, the femur can be felt to luxate in and out of the socket.

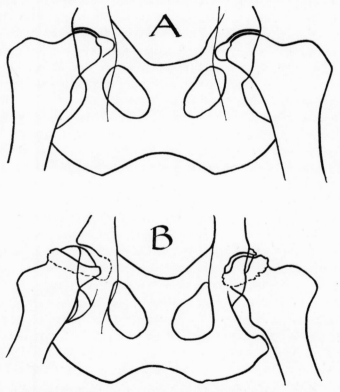

NORMAL HIP JOINTS
showing correct relationship of femoral heads & sockets

JOINTS SHOWING HIP DYSPLASIA
note alteration in relationship of femoral heads & sockets

Fig. 10 Normal joints and Hip Dysplasia

As changes take place with bone formation during the growing months of a young dog, it is considered wise to wait until after twelve months of age before subjecting the joints to X-ray. The Kennel Club have a scheme under which dogs can be X-rayed after twelve months and before six years and a form for X-raying under this scheme can be obtained from your Veterinary Surgeon, who can X-ray the dog and if satisfied with the result send it to the British Veterinary Association for consideration by a panel of scrutineers. Their decision will be that the dog's hips are: (1) Normal (2) They will send a Breeder's letter. This is to the effect that if all dogs with hips fractionally outside the limits laid down as Normal were not used for breeding then many other excellent qualities might be lost, but they advise that if the animal is to be bred it should be to a Normal dog. With any worse degree of trouble the result is (3) Failure.

A dog will make an excellent pet and may well go on for years without pain even if one or both joints are slightly affected, though it depends on the degree and whether it is progressive; usually muscles will develop and hold the joint in position. I know of one eight-year-old pet who can run or jump and does not appear a cripple though both joints are affected slightly. Of course he would not win prizes in the show ring as he moves with a kind of corkscrew movement and the hind legs work very close together, but he is happy and gives much pleasure to his family. In progressive cases and when arthritis sets in and causes pain, it is kindest to put the dog to sleep.

In America there are clinics where a technique of palpation is being used on puppies of about eight weeks to discover whether they are likely to be sound or dysplastic when X-rayed later on, and I understand they are finding a fair percentage of reliability in this method. This must be a great help to breeders.

The fact that the parents of a litter are X-rayed and found clear cannot be taken as a guarantee of perfection in the puppy, but statistics have proved that a much higher percentage of sound puppies are born from parents which are X-rayed and found clear, and when several generations have been clear of this trouble the percentage of affected puppies should be very small indeed.

Apart from the foregoing hereditary defects, the bobtail, like any other breed, can suffer from a variety of ailments and infections and my advice is to consult your Veterinary Surgeon without delay whenever the dog runs a temperature and is obviously feeling poorly.

The dog population has increased tremendously and every year there are epidemics of one kind or another and therefore vaccination of the puppy against the main infectious diseases is a necessity. This covers Hard pad and Distemper. In spite of being vaccinated, sometimes during an epidemic a dog can get a reaction, so that if the dog is off its food and appears poorly, coupled with a temperature and perhaps vomiting or diarrhoea, go at once for advice. The vaccination also covers Leptospirosis, of which there are two infections. One, attacking the liver and causing jaundice, is carried by rats and is not very common. The other, *Leptospirosis canicola*, which affects the kidneys, is more common especially among males. The dog will have a look of being tucked up at the loin and symptoms include vomiting and fever, also a great thirst.

Vaccination also covers Virus Hepatitis, which involves damage to the liver and symptoms include vomiting and diarrhoea and often haemorrhage. If you suspect any of the foregoing troubles seek Veterinary assistance at once. In most cases the vaccination will protect your dog, but sometimes it is still possible to pick up the infection.

ADMINISTERING PILLS AND MEDICINE

With one hand hold the top jaw with thumb one side and fingers the other and gently press it open. A pill should be put right at the back of the tongue and then pushed down the throat with the forefinger of the other hand. Holding the dog's mouth closed and keeping the nose pointing upward gently stroke the throat until the dog swallows. For medicine, put it in a small bottle and hold the dog's head with nose up high. Pour the medicine slowly and carefully in the side of the mouth making use of the slack part at the back of the lips as a kind of funnel, as shown in Fig. 11.

Fig. 11 Giving medicine

BAD BREATH

This may be caused by tartar forming on the teeth which often makes the gums inflamed. The tartar can be removed by use of a Zepto stick as already explained. Another cause of objectionable odour from the mouth is 'foul mouth' which is caused by bacteria in the crease or fold which is situated either side of the lower jaw. The hair should be cut off the part affected and a mild disinfectant used to bathe the area, then grease well to stop the saliva leaving it permanently damp.

DIARRHOEA

If the dog gets diarrhoea but seems otherwise in good

spirits and well, with no rise in temperature, it is probably a digestive upset. A light diet given in four small meals during the day and consisting of either white of egg with a dessert spoonful of glucose, scrambled egg with a little dry all bran, cornflour or arrowroot given as milk pudding (about ⅓ pint), will probably put things right. For a day or two keep the diet to scrambled egg or milk pudding or fish. At the same time remove the drinking water and allow the dog on the first day two tablespoonfuls of boiled water every hour or two as large draughts of water aggravate the position. As the dog improves the water can be increased until it is safe to return to normal drinking.

EAR INFLAMMATION

The bobtail has hair growing inside the ear and unless this is removed it will mat, especially if there is excessive wax, and the ear gets very sore and inflamed. Every week or two one should check the ears and attend to them when necessary as described in the chapter on grooming. If there is excessive irritation and the dog shakes his head and rubs the ears against things to show his discomfort, in spite of your attention to the ears, then it would appear he has more serious trouble and you should seek Veterinary advice.

ECLAMPSIA

This condition occurs at whelping time, though not often I am glad to say. The bitch will appear distressed and shivery and ultimately go into a coma, through lack of calcium. Immediate Veterinary attention is required if you are to save her life, but recovery is usually very fast once she has had an injection of a suitable calcium preparation.

FEET

Soreness between pads or cracked pads can be troublesome. Be sure the feet are properly trimmed between the pads, wipe clean with cotton wool and sprinkle with a little canker powder as this is very soothing.

GRASS SEEDS

Various grass seeds can penetrate the dog's skin and cause trouble. The worst of these is probably Wall Barley with its head of seeds each provided with an awn which makes the seed travel only one way – forward – causing a great amount of trouble particularly in a dry summer when the awn is dry and stiff. It can penetrate the dog's foot, ear, nose or even the vulva of a bitch, and once having entered it keeps travelling. A seed entering between the pads very often comes out above the toes or up the leg. Immediate veterinary attention is necessary especially if the seed is in the ear. The dog will suddenly begin shaking its head violently and persistently to try and rid itself of this thing which is pricking but each time he moves the seed works further in and one has to act very quickly to stop it disappearing towards the inner ear.

MASTITIS

When a bitch is suckling puppies there may be more milk than they need in the first few days, or they may neglect one teat and the milk glands become swollen, hard and painful. If you keep a watch for this happening any hardness and swelling can disappear if you put a strong puppy on the teat before real trouble begins. If neglected the bitch will probably go off her food, run a temperature and an abscess may form. Veterinary attention is necessary in this case.

OLD AGE

Once a dog is suffering and not enjoying life it is kind to have it put to sleep, but whilst it is enjoying life it has a right to happy retirement after a life of showing and breeding, or of being someone's constant companion. An older dog needs to be kept warmer than a youngster and if it gets pain and stiffness from rheumatism this can be eased by giving aspirin. It is not wise to give bones to an old dog to chew and therefore more attention will be needed to keep the teeth in order. Exercise should not be too strenuous in old age. I find the use of thinning scissors to reduce the coat of an old dog means less grooming is necessary – for very few old dogs enjoy having tangles combed out.

PARASITES

These fall into two groups : external and internal. As irritation from the presence of external parasites causes the dog to scratch and therefore plays havoc with the profuse coat of the bobtail, it is best to rely on prevention in the form of an occasional insecticidal shampoo or regular applications of insecticidal powder when attending to normal grooming.

In the case of the flea which lives on the body of the dog but comes off the dog to lay its eggs in the cracks of floor boards, etc., it is necessary to use insect powder in the kennel and on the bedding, as well as on the dog itself.

Lice stay on the body of the dog and the lice nits can be felt as small raised bumps on the dog's body. An insecticidal bath or use of insect powder is necessary with a further treatment about a week later in case new lice have hatched out.

Ticks can be picked up from grass where sheep graze and these bury their head under the dog's skin and only a little sack like portion can be seen sticking out and resembling a wart. It is important to make the tick release its hold before removing it or the head will stay behind and cause an abscess. A dab of surgical spirit or paraffin or petrol on the point of penetration will make the tick release its hold and with a piece of cotton wool or tissue the whole tick can be removed and burnt.

Harvest mites appear mostly on the ears or tummy or between the toes, and are picked up from the fields. They cause great irritation and the dog will bite himself and worry the affected part. These mites are tiny red insects and resemble small grains of red soil. It is simple to rid the dog of these with an application of insect powder.

Internal parasites: Round worms are present in most puppies and for this reason it is wise to give a worming dose whilst the puppies are three to six weeks old followed by a repeat dose two weeks later. Suitable worming medicine can be of a proprietary make or a dose can be obtained from your Veterinary Surgeon. A bitch can be wormed before being mated or when she is about two weeks in whelp to lessen the risk of her passing on worms to the puppies but it cannot ensure that the puppies will have no worms.

Tape worms are found in dogs of all ages and if neglected cause the dog to loose condition. Small white segments break off these worms, which are fixed by their heads to the intestines, and these segments can be seen in the faeces or around the anus. As the flea acts as an intermediary host by eating the eggs of the tapeworm, it is necessary to treat for fleas as well as tapeworm. It is advisable to obtain suitable worming tablets from your Veterinary Surgeon.

Hookworm is very rare in Britain but more common in North America. This type of worm is more difficult to diagnose as the only symptom is that the dog loses condition and does not thrive as it should. Veterinary attention is necessary.

SCRATCHING

First check for external parasites and if it is not that it may be due to the dog casting its coat, in which case you can assist by daily grooming to remove dead hair. It could also be due to the dog being over heated in which case put him on a light diet and give cooling powders.

TEMPERATURE

The thermometer used to take a dog's temperature can be similar to that used for humans but with a stubby 'blob-end' not a fragile one which might break off. The end of the thermometer should be lubricated with vaseline and inserted well into the rectum, and a 'half-minute' thermometer should be left there for one minute at least. The normal temperature of a dog is about 101.5°F.

13

BOBTAILS IN AMERICA

My first visit to America was in September 1972, when I had the pleasure of judging, first on the West coast in Northern and Southern California before crossing to judge at the Ox Ridge K.C. in the East. Thus I was afforded an opportunity to examine the show dogs on both sides of America and compare them with those at home. Also, I discovered at first hand the vast distances the majority of exhibitors travel in order to attend shows; distances covered by air travel which is fast and simple once in the 'plane, but necessitates being on time for the flight and crating the exhibits and seeing them loaded on and off, which is no easy task. Otherwise, it requires hours of fast highway driving. Both exhibitors and dogs must get very weary whichever way they choose to travel, though the enthusiasm and enterprise displayed has to be seen to be believed, and energy is unbounded.

In California the climate is hot and dry for months on end, especially in the Los Angeles area, and for this reason it is difficult to grow good coats on the dogs. Nature has taken a hand and good harsh coats are rare. There seems a problem with coats on the Eastern side also, for generally speaking the mature dogs have soft coats and this is puzzling because there were a number of youngsters with good coats coming. The best coat I handled was on a dog just over twelve months old. It would be interesting to see this dog in a year or two to find out whether he keeps the good, harsh texture.

America has such vastness and space and some quite un-

I

believable man-made wonders such as Golden Gate Park, which is an enormous parkland where there are trees, lakes and grassy areas, with room for every kind of sport. America has Disneyland which is delightful and fantastic and again shows vision, enthusiasm and ingenuity at its height. When it comes to dogs I have a feeling the breeders for the most part set to work with the same energy and drive to produce a dog that will win through to the top. Whilst striving to breed something that is really quality and top grade is an excellent goal, it is not as straightforward to breed a wonder dog as to complete a man-made wonder. Nature never did like to be hurried. A breeding programme usually takes years to accomplish and it needs care and planning and a great amount of luck as well.

The judges aim to judge twenty-five dogs per hour whereas in England we allow at least three minutes per dog. If a judge is hurried too much he has barely time to examine the dog thoroughly but must settle for a more superficial look, so that a clever handler may gloss over a fault. Rather drastic trimming has come into practice and I feel many rears lost their full beauty of width and height by being over shaped, presumably to accentuate shortness of body. Legs are trimmed to cover up lack of angulation, etc., but if a keen judge is allowed time to feel what is under the trimmed coat he will not be deceived. I only hope they do not run into too much trouble with this practice of trimming. If one has an exhibit with cow hocks or lack of angulation the plan should be to take time and breed something that does not have to have its shape altered, rather than hide it up and win. Winners are so likely to be used to reproduce more stock with the same fault.

This practice of trimming is more obvious in the Eastern region, where they seem to have bred for excellent skulls, but in the Western region the trimming idea is creeping in and there I saw several dogs presumably done hastily by novices with obvious scissor chopping, which looks terrible.

I feel very strongly that the desire to 'hasten' everything is at the root of the trouble. Hurry to win, hurry to judge, hurry to put a puppy or youngster in the Open class even if it could appear earlier, to get points, and hurry to be a Champion. Unlike our entries in England, it is unusual to get an exhibit in more than one class. They bring puppies out and hurry till they get the points for Champion and then can only appear with the Champions in the Best of Breed class where Champion Dogs and Bitches appear together with the Best of Winners and Reserve Best of Winners from the previous classes.

In England we often discuss whether Champions should continue to be shown as long as their owners please or whether there should be a limit on the number of times they come out as Champions, but as the system is at present the competition is hard and no one races a young dog through but takes time entering in appropriate classes and thus these early classes are competitive and well filled. On the other hand, in America early classes are very poorly supported as they feel a need to enter in the Open Class to be noticed enough to gain points, and this seems a pity.

There is a marked difference in type between bobtails in the Eastern and the Western regions, with the East providing very good skulls – in some cases massive skulls – and dogs there were generally squarely built. However, there were not enough with good neck and shoulders and the correct pear-shaped body; also many of the exhibits were very much overweight as if they mistakenly substituted fatness for substance. In California there is more elegance, especially where necks and shoulders are concerned and it needs a breeding programme to include the great skulls and shorter bodies from the New York area. All the breeders in both regions should strive for coat improvement. I noticed that the harsh coat, if it began to appear, was not cherished by the use of whalebone or bristle brushes. There is widespread use of wire brushes and these are too severe and break off the top coat.

This may accentuate the difference in Britain where the use of pin brushes is frowned upon. In addition, of course, the climate is on the side of the British breeder.

With the distinct separation of type between East and West in America, one realises that the vast distance involved is much of the reason, whereas the British bobtails have progressed more slowly over the years and there has been a gradual merging of bloodlines and this has produced a more uniform breed. The majority of British bobtails have reasonable or good coats both for colour and texture and many are exceptionally good. Normally our dogs progress gradually to full bloom when they are three or four years old, and whilst there is obviously a certain amount of variety, it is not anything like the sharp division of type seen in America.

At the shows I attended and judged there were a number of professional handlers in the Eastern region and a very few in the West, whereas in Britain in Old English Sheepdogs professional handlers are non-existent and we all like to bring up our stock in our own way and show them ourselves. It is interesting that I discovered later that my Best of Breed at the three shows I judged were not professionally handled.

The bobtail has sprung into popularity too quickly in all countries and consequently there are not sufficient judges who are experienced in the breed to officiate. All-breed judges in America tend to move the dogs in the ring at a very fast pace rather like the German Shepherd dog, and they do not seem to realise that for bobtails a lively pacing known as the 'characteristic ambling' movement is desirable. In Britain our judges wisely require both this amble and a faster movement. If the show ring is large enough, they very often request a gallop as well! As a working dog, the bobtail should be able to keep up a steady, springy amble behind a flock of sheep, should have a faster pace behind cattle and always be ready to produce a turn of great speed – the elastic 'gallop' – to overtake an animal that has broken away.

The hospitality extended to myself and my husband was

just wonderful; organisers were kind and helpful and set out
to entertain us, to introduce us to other club members and to
show us something of the surroundings. At home I feel we
could learn something from their wholehearted approach
and from their enterprise. The ring at Ox Ridge was dec-
orated with tubs of chrysanthemums and looked most attractive, and they arranged to have a video tape recording of
the complete judging, accompanied by an excellent commen-
tary and this caused great interest.

As the summer shows do not have benching, exhibitors
tend to gather under brightly coloured awnings and tents,
and to box their exhibits in big cages which also serve as
travelling kennels for air travel. The spacious settings with
these little encampments around the ring, plus the numerous
campers and large vans parked around the showground,
produce very much of a garden party atmosphere.

I saw some good bobtails on both East and West sides of
America and it would be an advantage if there were a merging of bloodlines. If only breeders and exhibitors would use
patience in all programmes it would be a good thing. I know
their enthusiasm and energy is unbounded and they are
capable of attempting anything but there are no short cuts
with a breeding programme. For instance, in working to
establish a really first class coat, they should try to include
all the other attributes necessary for a top quality, sound bobtail and never fail to remember above all that this is a working breed. The dog that is required should be powerful
enough to keep of marauders, built for endurance and with
agility enough to do a day's work.

It was a pleasure to have the opportunity to meet so many
exhibitors and dogs and the whole trip was packed with
interest and enjoyment.

Appendix

OLD ENGLISH SHEEPDOG CLUBS

OLD ENGLISH SHEEPDOG CLUB (Founded 1888)

Secretary:
Mrs I. Lapwood,
9 Highfield Road,
Northwood, Middlesex.

NORTH WESTERN OLD ENGLISH SHEEPDOG CLUB (Founded 1922)

Hon. Secretary:
Miss D. Brocklesby,
85 Bentley Road,
Doncaster, Yorkshire.

OLD ENGLISH SHEEPDOG CLUB OF SCOTLAND (Founded 1932)

Hon. Secretary:
Mr G. K. Leslie,
105 Meadowhouse Road,
Edinburgh.

SOUTH EASTERN OLD ENGLISH SHEEPDOG CLUB (Founded 1946)

Hon. Secretary:
Mrs C. Masterson,
43 The Avenue,
Gravesend, Kent.

OLD ENGLISH SHEEPDOG CLUB OF WALES (Founded 1965)

Hon. Secretary:
Mrs G. Mogford,
Brynawelon,
Risca, Monmouthshire.